BLUFF YOUR WAY IN MARKETING

GRAHAM HARDING
&
PAUL WALTON

Ravette London

Published by Ravette Limited
3 Glenside Estate, Star Road,
Partridge Green, Horsham,
Sussex RH13 8RA
(0403) 710392

Series Editor — Anne Tauté

Cover design — Jim Wire
Typesetting — Reprotype
Printing & Binding — Cox & Wyman Ltd.
Production — Oval Projects Ltd.

The Bluffer's Guides are based on
an original idea by Peter Wolfe.

CONTENTS

Diagrams:

THE MARKETING CONCEPT

Marketing activity involves taking something simple and obvious and sticking it in fancy packaging. This is a skill all good bluffers quickly learn.

The idea of marketing itself is no exception. In lay terms the marketing concept means that you stand a better chance of flogging something if you understand whether and why someone wants it in the first place. But to the marketing man, The Marketing Concept is very serious stuff, as important as The Meaning of Life. In fact, to heavy-duty marketeers it *is* the meaning of life and the best bluffers will show a reverence towards it which echoes a lawyer's belief in the rule of law or a doctor's in the Hippocratic Oath.

The marketing concept is to be differentiated in business strategy from a number of other misguided and inferior approaches.

The Production Concept: Produce what we sell

This an immensely inward-looking, technology-worshipping approach which can easily produce better mousetraps that nobody wants to buy.

The Sales Concept: Sell what we produce

This is a slightly more evolved view of business and accordingly is either staggeringly successful or absolutely catastrophic. Its ruling classes are the salesmen.

The Trading Concept

This consists of buying a little, selling a little and making a little.

As a well-read bluffer in marketing, you will recognise lower forms of business orientation and demonstrate the superiority of the marketing concept at every possible moment.

A good stratagem for bluffers in meetings where people temorarily forget what marketing is about, is to trot out a suitably learned homily for reminding your audience about the magic of the marketing concept.

A few maxims for marketeers would include the following:

★ "Marketing is human activity directed at satisfying needs and wants through exchange processes." — P. Kotler. Boring but sound.

★ "The job of the marketeer is to get the best fit between company resources and consumer needs." — J. H. Davidson. Good with non-marketing colleagues.

★ "Marketing is disciplined demand management." Particularly useful when your marketing director is more interested in your advertising than he is in your volume forecasts.

★ "The purpose of marketing is to earn a profit by adding the maximum value at the minimum cost." — C. McIver. Very useful in Agency negotiations when they submit some outlandish production invoice.

★ "Marketing is the intelligence service of the corporate army." — Anon. Care should be used in deploying this on the basis that military intelligence is a contradiction in terms.

Then there is the cocktail party question: "And what do *you* do?". More often than not, you will have to defend yourself against accusations of using all manner of techniques to persuade the consumer (i.e. everyone else in the room) to buy products they don't need by the use of expensive advertising that they have to pay for.

The argument that marketing is a humanistic philosophy, making the consumer the centre of the universe, will not wash with clever lawyers, jealous accountants or left wing intellectuals who can smell blood.

The best bluffers will avoid any introduction of

themselves containing the word marketing. Much safer gambits are:

   Business (mysterious — trading? the City?)
   Sausages (on second thoughts, perhaps not)
   Research (nicely ambiguous but avoid this one with
       academics in the room)
   General Management (sounds impressive)
   Industry (sound but boring).

Good bluffers resist the temptation to explain the ways of the marketing world to the masses. The media's only interest in marketing is making good television out of marketing men's discomfort. You have been warned.

Marketing As Warfare

Unless you're a pacifist, treat marketing as war. It doesn't matter whether it's war against your colleagues, war against your suppliers, war against your channels of distribution or war against your competitors. War is a good metaphor for the business of marketing.

You can discuss frontal assaults, pincer movements, guerilla warfare. You can talk of shock troops, supply chains, tactical withdrawals, the chain of command.

Best of all for serious bluffers is the art of war — Japanese style. The classic text is Miyamoto Musashi's *A Book of Five Rings*. This 17th century Teach Yourself strategy for samurai contains all the budding international marketeer need ever know about making his or her way in the world. For example:

   "In all forms of strategy it is necessary to maintain the combat stance in everyday life and to make your everyday stance your combat stance".

   "In strategy it is important to see distant things as if they were close and to take a distanced view of close things".

7

"Suppress the enemy's useful actions but allow his useless actions".

Whilst you are putting up this smokescreen you should not neglect the Home Front. Establish a reputation for inside information. Manoeuvre for position with your boss. Lastly, consider the assignments that will bring glory without unnecessary exposure to risk.

Marketing Men's Neuroses

Marketing men are prone to several complexes and good bluffers will know about them. In certain cases they will be *affected* so as to look the part properly, in others *sublimated* to avoid being cast as villain of the piece or sacked. So care is needed in applying this knowledge.

Integration

What marketeers mean by 'integration' is that marketing has to be the top-gun in the boardroom. Not everyone shares this view.

As young marketing trainees discover — life is not pure Kotler and there are many companies where marketing is neither the centre of the universe nor the centre of the 'organisational wheel'. In fact there are many companies where the chairman's wife or the motorcycle couriers are more 'integrated' than the marketing department.

The lessons for successful marketing bluffers are:

a) **Understand the 'culture' of the company**
This is a trendy way of saying who runs the company and who sets the house rules. It could be 'marketing' or a marketeer. It might just as well be:

Sales	The Family
Finance	The Chairman
Production	The Chairman's Mistress
R & D	The Chairman's Hitman
The Typing Pool	

In a sales dominated business, you should write their scripts, show lots of energy, be part of the 'solution', never 'part of the problem', show interest (but not too much) in their customers and have plenty of action plans. Do not waste your time trying to sell them marketing as the Harvard Business School teaches it, unless you are mentally retarded, a masochist or both.

b) **Acknowledge that what marketing is and what marketing men do are different things**
As many marketeers demonstrate every day, you do not have to know what marketing is to work in the marketing department.

If you find yourself in a company where marketing is not central and where your boss thinks the Boston Matrix is a wrestling hold, do not despair. If it suits you, have fun enjoying the pleasant things that marketing men do like awaydays and trips to the Agency. If it doesn't suit you, spend your time constructively polishing your CV for eventual relaunch into a more heavy duty marketing situation.

At all costs do not be neurotic about integration unless the culture is.

Selling

Because marketing is currently in vogue, everybody is getting into it. In popular usage, marketing has come to mean selling with a college education, as in:

Marketing Area	Done by
Property marketing	Estate agents, Timeshare sharks
Energy Conservation Marketing	Double Glazing companies
Financial Services Marketing	Life Insurance companies

When you are confronted with someone who confuses your role with selling, the best strategy is to suggest that you are as much involved in selling as Shakespeare was in acting, or, if in the company of other marketeers, suggest that good marketing makes selling unnecessary. Yet another stratagem is to agree wholeheartedly, saying "Yes, of course, I'm in the business of selling ideas". It's called repositioning yourself as a Communications Consultant.

The Diffusion of Marketing and The Marketing of Diffusion

Diffusion is what most marketing men believe happened to cult objects such as Porsche, Filofax and (briefly) Fosters.

What you have to do is get your product adopted by the trend-setters and spend such money you have on persuading them of its exclusivity. Then, so the idea runs, it will spread from its original niche in Covent Garden wine bars or Los Angeles racquet clubs to the lesser breeds of today's acquisitive society. And you will make money.

The successful bluffer will argue cogently that it's quite possible to diffuse too fast.

The other key thing to know about diffusion is that, technically speaking, it's the diffusion *curve* that's the important thing.

The Diffusion of Innovations

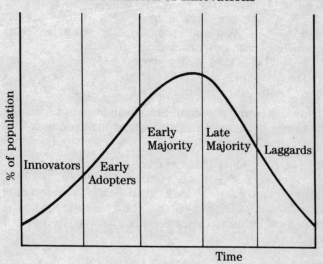

You affect to be one of the early majority ('a man of the people') but you will wish others to see you as either an innovator or as one of the early adopters, the trend watchers, and will act accordingly. On no account should you be seen as one of the late majority or, God forbid, one of the laggards.

The great thing about diffusion from the bluffer's point of view is that *everything* (products, people, regions of the country, attitudes, illnesses, companies, even whole industries) can be skewered neatly on the curve.

Take marketing itself for example:

The innovators were the American **FMPG** companies who adopted marketing in the 1950s. Procter and Gamble were one of the first and are still one of the best of the 'blue-chip' marketing companies.

The early majority — in the 1960s — included the drinks and beverages companies. They've stayed pretty good at it, but you might score by suggesting they're increasingly reactive rather than 'proactive'.

In the 1970s the retailers discovered marketing; computer companies thought they had. For evidence that they hadn't you need only cite their inability to:

a) create any powerful brands and
b) recognise user benefits rather than product benefits.

The late majority in the marketing ball were the financial services companies who came piling in, in the 1980s. You need only cite the indistinguishable TV advertising (conducted for the benefit of Oxbridge satirists) and the paucity of branding in insurance ads to prove the obvious cliches about the late majority.

The laggards include politics and publishing, only now waking up to marketing. Following the American example, British politicians have polished the image of their parties, thrown themselves headlong into direct mail and embraced the market research and positioning paraphernalia of marketing companies. Unkindly, one might say that the problem is the basic products.

Turning a problem into an opportunity (as all marketeers should) you will see that the route to power and success in marketing is to take the gospel to one of the laggards. Marketing is now given lip service in big financial institutions but there still many businesses where a little marketing bluff will take you a long way.

SPEAKING THE LANGUAGE

Marketing, like many other new professions, has an extensive cloud of unknowing hanging over it. This takes the form of jargon. You deplore the over-use of jargon but this should not stop you using it for all you're worth.

Rule 1: Always refer to the market in which you operate in terms which are incomprehensible to any literate outsider:

Never		*Always*
Butter and margarine	—	Yellow Fats
Radios, TVs etc.	—	Brown Goods
Washing machines, fridges etc.	—	White Goods
Spuds	—	White Veg
Toothpaste	—	Oral hygiene/Dentrifices
Bars of chocolate	—	Countlines

Rule 2: Complicate rather than simplify:

Never		*Always*
Reasons for buying	—	Composite Explanatory Variables
Idea	—	Concept
Good Idea	—	Key concept
Bad idea	—	Interesting concept
Disagree	—	Play Devil's Advocate
Gradual	—	Evolutionary
New	—	Revolutionary
What we're going to do	—	Strategy

Rule 3: Turn the obvious questions on their heads. Do not ask "Is there a gap in the market?" Ask, as Bernstein does, "Is there a market in the gap?". Not "What's the problem?" but "Where's the opportunity in the problem?"

MARKETING GURUS

Marketing, like all pseudo-professions, takes its academic gunslingers very seriously.

It is definitely useful to know a little about marketing's Hot Gospellers and indeed it is very fashionable to beachcomb for interesting bits of conceptual flotsam and jetsam washed up at conferences. But deploy such learning with care: the best way of concept dropping is with a degree of cynicism. Most marketing men have a love-hate relationship with clever thinking. They love their own and hate everybody else's.

Here are small number of carefully chosen gurus with a note on their work.

Theodore Levitt

Levitt (or Ted, if you want to impress your audience and suggest the excellence of your marketing credentials) has been intimately associated with the Harvard Business Review (HBR to the intiated) and is a leading professor at the school. He is probably the most able apologist of the Marketing Concept, and the skilled bluffer should nod approvingly of two seminal Levitt texts: *Marketing Myopia* (HBR, 1960) and *The Globalisation of Markets* (HBR, 1983).

Marketing Myopia is an essential piece of conceptualisation for all bluffers. It originated from Levitt's analysis of the decline and fall of the great American railroads. These suffered from myopia because they saw themselves as being in the railway business rather than the transportation business and so let all manner of new competitors steal their customers.

The principle of marketing myopia allows you to look quite impressive in meetings. In a serious development meeting, ask your colleagues what business they are in. For example, supposing you work in marketing for a

bank, possible answers to the question could be:
1. Banking.
   This should have been anticipated but keep at it anyway.
2. Retailing.
   An interesting possibility — but a short term one, perhaps.
3. Information Technology.
   Make the clever so and so who said this say what it actually means.
4. Dreams (via credit and loans).
   Encourage this participant.
5. 'Security' for *people*.
   This one will definitely go the distance. Watch out for your job.

Philip Kotler

Always referred to as 'Kotler' as in 'Roget's' or 'Wisden' but without the rude words of the former or the wit of the latter. You should claim to have read Kotler at some stage in your career because his not-so-slim volume is the standard vademecum for marketing students.

Kotler is sound but sedating. Only in *Marketing Management: Analysis, Planning and Control* will you find such classics as:

★ Demarketing
★ Counter Marketing
★ Synchromarketing
★ Remarketing

Whatever they are.

Igor Ansoff

Another useful name to drop especially when discussing **New Product Development (NPD)**. Ansoff is the author of *Corporate Strategy*, an immensely unreadable text with one or two good pictures. His diversification matrix differentiates between existing products and new products; and between existing markets and new markets. Putting the two together can provide hours of fun at awaydays.

Ansoff's Diversification Matrix

Product		
Existing		New
Existing Market	Penetration	Product Development
New Market	Line	Diversification Extension

Michael Porter
Another Harvard man reinforcing their dominant share in the marketing guru business. Porter is a specialist in analysing competitive forces. *Competitive Strategy* (1980) and *Competitive Advantage* (1985) will look good (i.e. intimidating) on your office shelves.

J. H. (Hugh) Davidson
A home grown guru, with a blue-chip CV in the practice of marketing and a very nice line in aggressive marketing tactics. His recently reissued manifesto, *Offensive Marketing*, is a marvellous initiation for marketing virgins. Bluffers of a certain age will of course claim to have read the first edition — "when it came out". (That means hardback in 1972 or Penguin in 1975.)

MARKETING TYPES

There are three basic types of marketeers (and some of them are very basic). Type 1 is the Academic. Type 2 is Action Man. Type 3 the Street Trader. The problem is to decide which type is going to work best for you. Qualifications are irrelevant, as is knowledge. It's the conviction with which you play the role that's crucial.

The Academic

Regardless of educational background, you should behave as if you went to Oxford or Cambridge. Because so many marketing men *did* go to Oxbridge it's dangerous to make too precise a claim. You will have studied History or English or Modern languages, possibly a science subject — but not Economics.

You should read the marketing press openly and keep clippings from obscure (or American) marketing journals above your desk. You have, of course, read *In Search of Excellence* but you know that its sequel *A Passion for Excellence* is better because it's more "action-orientated".

The academic marketing man doesn't *do* things (at least not without much research and many feasibility studies) but he is proud to be action-orientated. As an academic bluffer you will also have read the popular classics of business life like *The Peter Principle, Up the Organisation* and *Further up the Organisation*. You will, however, be less open about these particular works and pass off their practical wisdom as your own "insights".

You dress well (a penchant for bow-ties is acceptable), drive a Series 3 BMW and, if the conversation turns to sporting pastimes, admit to having fenced a little at college or played a spot of Real Tennis — but not recently. When you take holidays — which you may do

17

frequently — you make it clear that they are taken not for the sake of entertainment or relaxation *per se* but to "recharge your creative batteries". Your heroes are Levitt and Porter and you will refer to them as your "mentors".

A sub-grouping of the academic is the **strategist**. The strategist shares most of the same behavioural traits as the academic but tends to be less showy and more addicted to smoking a pipe.

As a strategist you should constantly ask your colleagues (and superiors) whether a particular action meets the agreed strategic objectives (never the strategy). Since there's a good chance that most people won't remember their corporate objectives (let alone their business mission) you score highly. All you need to know is that the actions of those who can help you and your career are 'on strategy'. The rest aren't.

You can bolster the impact of your questions by citing obscure analogies from military history. "Is this the Somme in early 1916?", you will enquire, "or perhaps the Sino-Manchurian conflict of 1905?". This is guaranteed to leave everyone else silent — particularly those who trained as historians — and the field will be clear to draw your own conclusions.

But beware of too many definite answers. Strategy is about long-term issues not short-term action. Your hero may well be the Duke of Wellington: monosyllabic, down to earth and intolerant of fools.

The Action Man

Action man's credo was best summed up by William Casey, American millionaire, spymaster and conspirator: 'Set tasks. Set deadlines. Make decisions. Act. Get it done and move on'.

Education and background are irrelevant — except that the successful bluffer must acquire a curt and heavyweight style of memo writing and the ability to delegate all the tasks to someone else. As action man, you set the tasks and the deadlines. You take a great many decisions and take credit for a great deal of action. You then move on. This is crucial. Stay in one job a fraction too long and the consequences of the decisions and the actions may catch up. The results could be dire.

Publicly you don't read the marketing press — you have no time. Instead you require your subordinates to go through the press with a hi-liter — a useful familiarisation exercise you feel and one which is done solely for their benefit. In private you read the job advertisements with attention.

If you allow yourself one piece of familiarity with the business gurus it may well be Peter Drucker's claim that 'concentration is the key to economic results'. Or, in the words of Peters and Waterman, 'stick to the knitting'.

When you entertain you do so at smart but 'newly discovered' restaurants. You don't have time for holidays — except the occasional weekend skiing in Tahoe or windsurfing in Corsica. Your heroes are entrepreneurs like John Egan and Ralph Halpern. For these people — who will normally be much older and much more senior than you — and for these people *only* you will have "a lot of time". But not *too* much.

The Street Trader

Much the most difficult for the would-be bluffer. You must have left school early — preferably after organising some highly profitable (and slightly dodgy) activity from the local telephone box. Ideally, you will have started with a barrow in Petticoat Lane, certainly you ascribe your success to a talent for trading. You will have made your way up from rags to riches (exaggerate both) by exercise of a powerful personality and a talent for spotting opportunities.

You should pay absolutely no attention to market research or marketing theory. Your instinct (call it your "gut feeling") is what counts. You would, you say, much prefer to be out in the field selling or talking to the customers, than behind a desk. This provides the justification for a generous expense account which you spend on late night entertainment for customers.

Your clothes are largely irrelevant but are certainly different from those of your colleagues. When you've made it you will pilot your own helicopter. Until then you drive whatever comes to hand with a blatant disregard for other road users.

Your philosophy of marketing (which will be immediately obvious from what you do, rather than what you say) is to pile it high, make a lot of noise and sell it cheap. You won't care much about exactly what product you're dealing with but you will threaten to knock the block off anyone who makes unfavourable comments about it. You will reserve your greatest contempt for wimps of any variety. In your early days your holidays will be spent running another business on the side. This will probably make (or have already made) your first million. In later life you'll have the time and energy to get into highly conspicuous consumption.

Your heroes are men like Richard Branson and Alan Sugar. You'll know (and quote) Sugar's remark that whereas other companies love and care for the customer 'at Amstrad we want your money'. You'll also know that Amstrad derives quite simply from Alan Michael Sugar Trading. That's where you're heading. Get it right and you'll not only do it but make a great deal of money for those sharp enough to spot how good you are. Including yourself.

THE MARKETING HIERARCHY

Managing Director/General Manager — Somebody who has transcended mere marketing into the upper management ether. Still likes to get involved occasionally — usually with your advertising. Treat with apparent respect.

Marketing Director — Usually your boss and the board member responsible for all marketing activities and personnel. Very popular with the Royal Mail due to the pile of love letters delivered daily from Advertising Agencies.

Director of Marketing — Deceptively similar to the above but not on the board of the company. In marketing jargon, a question mark or problem child.

Marketing Controller — Someone with the talent of a Marketing Manager and the vanity of a Marketing Director. Usually sublimates his aggression into your expenses and the questioning thereof.

Marketing Manager — Group Product Manager with go-faster stripes.

Marketing Operations Manager — Invaluable ally or dangerous enemy. The person who makes sure everything happens on time, at the right price, and in the best hotels.

Brand Manager — Either the storm troopers of marketing or the Thin Red Line. 'Brand masochists' is another description.

Assistant Brand Manager — An endangered species. The position no one ever admits to. Who would want to be an *assistant* oily rag?

Marketing Assistant — Graduate trainee with sales experience.

Graduate Trainee — Enthusiast with no experience. Usually the best informed about such trivia as sales volumes, customers, etc. This is because they're still keener on their jobs than their careers.

Marketing And Its Interfaces

There are two sets of people to consider here. Those inside the company and those outside.

The Insiders

As a marketeer you see yourself at the centre of the organisational wheel. That goes without saying — though you recognise that there are still plenty of corporate luddites who don't see things your way.

The argument runs like this. Business is about meeting the needs of customers — at a profit. Therefore the customers and their needs must be at the centre of any profitable approach to business. Support for this view comes from Hugh Davidson who defined marketing as the 'total approach to business which places the consumer at the centre of things'. Two other good quotes are: "Markets don't pay bills, customers do" and "Customers make pay day possible". Thus you should be setting the strategy, you should be controlling the production and directing the sales people and the accountants should be advising you on how to do so profitably.

Unfortunately they don't usually see it that way. Conflict is the name of the game — it's called office politics.

The conflict with **Sales** is usually the bitterest. This is because it's a class issue. It used to be secondary modern kids against the grammar school swots. Now it's more likely to be technical college versus university. In a year or so it will probably be university versus Business school types.

You have two courses of action with sales people:

1. Be publicly aggressive and privately one of the lads. This should enable you to get away unscathed with dirty deeds.

2. Advocate the integration of sales and marketing. This is shorthand for marketing telling the sales people what to do — but "integration" sounds better.

Dealing with **Production** is less of a problem. Nobody pays them very much attention because nobody these days wants to be thought a 'product-led' company. This can be a dangerous attitude. Quality control and technical feasibility are very important to any marketing concept when it hits the real world. You should insist that your people "take pride in the product" and — in public at least — you should do so yourself. It will win you a lot of points and it should make the production director your ally (which can be a very good thing indeed).

Active conflict with the **Accountants** is dangerous. Corporate finance directors still carry a lot of clout — particularly in subsidiary companies whose ultimate owners have a lot of expensive paper washing round the Stock Market.

In private you can dismiss them as 'bean-counters' and point to the ineptitude of the American car industry in front of Japanese competition as an example of what happens when accountants get their inky fingers on the levers of power.

In public adopt the 'hard man'/'soft man' approach. On the one hand beat them over the head with reams of market research data. On the other appeal to their entrepreneurial instincts (if they have any). Go for the Big

Idea. Even if you don't convince the accountants you'll impress everyone else.

Finally, two groups of in-house people you must always have on your side:

1. **Secretaries** — invaluable for last minute typing, fixing impossible meetings, providing inside information on the boss's state of mind, fending off unwanted phone calls, booking the best hotels and bending the rules.
2. Whoever has the key to the corporate cocktail cabinet.

The Outsiders

Agencies present one sort of problem; you have to pay them.

Agencies range from good to awful but this doesn't make much difference to their price — particularly if you're operating on a commission basis. (The theory was, and still is, that the agency costs you nothing because they get a discount on the media space they buy for you, and then charge you the same amount as their commission. If you believe that you'll believe anything.)

The important thing is to get the *best* available operators and get the *most* out of them. They exist to serve you. Remember that. This doesn't necessarily mean that they will do what you want but they should always be prepared to humour your incidental wishes on the subject of good contacts, lunch, entertainment, introductions to dishy secretaries or smooth young account men, alternative jobs and so forth. They may even be willing to hire you.

The one exception to this rule is market research agencies. Ethics, professional codes of conduct and less money mean they don't appear such an accommodating bunch. There are three things to remember about marketing research agencies:

1. Make sure they know what results you expect before they start work (or at least before they write their reports).
2. Insist that there is a 'management summary' at the front of the report. (This should definitely say what you want them to say.)
3. Ensure they put the unwanted bits somewhere around page 297. Nobody will ever see them there.

Consumers and **customers** present another sort of problem. You have to get them to pay you.

Consumers are the subject of fascinated study by armies of marketeers, market research companies and advertising agencies. You need to be aware of what 'real' people are currently doing and thinking. This is the justification — if any were needed — for reading the *Sun*, watching EastEnders, studying the Agony columns or the letters pages of men's magazines, buying bottles of champagne or Marks & Spencer's ready meals. Whatever takes your fancy in fact. The trick is to ensure that all such diversions go down on your expenses sheet as 'product samples' or 'market research' expenses.

Qualitative research groups are always a source of good consumer anecdotes. It may help you to know, for example, that Tesco shoppers are always more outgoing, more friendly and much funnier than Sainsbury shoppers. That 17 year old Glaswegian headbangers know more about the contents and containers of every conceivable form of alcohol than you ever will.

Customers may also be consumers. But not necessarily. More often than not *customers* are retailers and *their* customers are your consumers. Not everyone has caught up with this obvious fact. Not everyone has got used to new ways of dealing with customers.

Consumer marketing used to be the focus of manufacturers' marketing activity. But now retailers like Safeway, Habitat and Next have established their own branded identities and the new idea is Trade Marketing.

Trade marketing is about applying the same standard of research, rigour and creativity to the trade, as old-style marketing departments did to the consumer. Having applied that effort, the challenge is to create long-term relationships with the trade in the same way as Lever Brothers did with its Persil mums. That means understanding the needs of the trade and getting away from relationships that are based solely on today's special offer. They don't last.

Tell anyone who insists on low prices to remember 'winners compete by delivering a product that supplies superior values to customers rather than one that costs less'.

Above all, avoid the trap of Marketing Myopia. Think 'customers' rather than 'consumers' when it comes to developing new products, assessing communication channels or commissioning research.

An associated trap is Consumerism. Don't believe everything consumers say to you. Some of the most successful product launches have been those which flew in the face of all the research evidence — and vice versa.

If you're launching a new product you can always claim that consumers are slow to appreciate something they don't already know about. Conversely, score points by asking "Where's the real product difference?" Research on NPD does show that if the product does not have such a difference, its chances are pretty slim. It all goes to prove that the big idea is best.

WHAT MARKETEERS DO

1. Develop Market Plans

Marketeers, like politicians, come in a variety of hues and views. And just as all politicians have to face election from time to time, marketeers have to get through marketing plans. These activities are in fact very similar — both involve rehashing the past and over-promising the future.

The future is very important to marketing, something which sets it aside from finance. Superficially, a marketing plan is a bit like a balance sheet or profit and loss account, but whilst the P & L and balance sheet are snapshots relating to the past, the marketing plan is a vision of the future.

It is easy to get excited about a vision of the future — especially when it happens to be yours — but always remember that visions stretch credibility, especially with Chief Executives who have seen it all before. Be very careful with the 'expansiveness of your perspective'.

Marketing plans come in a number of guises:

★ Annual Brand Plan
★ Market Strategy
★ Budget

and will have varying time horizons:

1 year/2 years/3 years/5 years/10 years.

The longer the range of a plan, the longer the odds on anybody taking it seriously.

Marketing plans also bring out different things in marketing people. Action men hate the annual navel-gazing activity as much as the more academic love to work up a sweat with a **SWOT chart** or a juicy little **matrix.**

Most marketing textbooks will tell you that good planning only emerges from rigorous analysis of the key questions about the business. But what bluffers should be asking are:

The Open Questions	The Hidden Questions
Where are we now?	For a start, why am *I* here now?
How did we get there?	Who is to blame and why has he got a bigger car?
Where do we want to be?	Never mind "we". Where do *I* want to be?
How do we get there?	How do I get my CV typed without the boss seeing it?

Marketing planning depends on a number of key concepts. The chief one is:

Segmentation

Remember, 'If you're not thinking segments, you're not thinking marketing'. Ted Levitt said that. It's worth remembering. This does not mean dismembering your Marketing Director into his component parts — tempting though that may be.

The consumers in a market, any market, have different needs which can be satisfied by different products or different positionings of similar (or even identical) products. Split your market into groups of customers:

★ by age
★ by life-cycle stage (an impressive way of talking about the differences between, say, those who are married and those who are not)
★ by attitudes to using credit cards, or

★ by any combination of the above and a hundred other attributes.

Instantly you have a segmentation. You are limited only by your imagination and that of your agency.

Agencies (or rather their planning departments) compete for new and more 'focused' (read elaborate) segmentations of each and every market.

You should know that Hugh Davidson describes segmentation as a 'touchstone for offensive marketing'. Segmentation is a powerful tool for:

★ new product development
★ maximising the potential of existing brands and
★ avoiding cannibalisation (winning sales at your expense rather than that of your competitors).

But beware of segmenting the market so finely that you finish up with a host of separate market sectors that are too small to attack profitably.

Key segmentation variables are:

a) demographics
b) usage level, and
c) personality or lifestyle factors (don't use the word psychographic unless your ambition is to be thought intellectual *and* old fashioned).

Some people would include value — effectively a segmentation around various price points — but this does not help to *understand* the market.

There are two key questions to ask of any segmentation.

1. Does this segmentation help us to understand our customers better and market to them more effectively?
2. Is the segmentation supported by data? Listen hard to the answers for the sounds of evasive action.

The Product Life-Cycle

The easy way of explaining why your sales are disappearing. That's the defensive use. The offensive use is to ask what stage of its life-cycle a given product has reached. Whatever the answer ignore it and ask about the **product portfolio mix** *(q.v.)*.

You'll know, of course, that it's based on the sensible and realistic idea that every product goes through:

a) a period of development (high costs, low revenue and low profit)

b) a period of growth (rapidly rising sales and profits)

c) a period of maturity (highest sales but declining profit margin as competitors come in and prices tend to fall) and finally

d) a period of decline (consumers shift to new products, competition intensifies, sales and profits drop right away).

You will also know — and gently point out — that it seems that nobody told Mars about it. Or Kellogs. Or Heinz. Or a number of other marketing-centred companies that know the value of powerful brands.

Products certainly have a life-cycle. Brands needn't have. Even the seemingly moribund can be renewed and repositioned. You can quote the case history of Lucozade as a perfect example of this truism. From being the old fashioned bedside tonic for invalids it became — with Daley Thompson's assistance — the teenage energy drink of the 80s. Recovery indeed.

New brands are very hard to create which explains why shrewd operators like Lord Hanson and John Elliott are willing to spend a lot of money on buying old brands. A good question to ask about anybody's brands — except your own — is "But are they *real* brands?". Very often they aren't.

30

Portfolio Planning

This, as all strategically minded bluffers know very well, used to be very sexy stuff indeed: "a major task of top management". It provided the excuse for elegant matrices and made a *lot* of money for the Boston Consulting Group. It's still pretty powerful and you should appear to know all about it.

Business or brands are plotted against the twin axes of market growth rate and relative market share. You therefore get four quadrants — each with its complement of **SBUs (Strategic Business Units):**

Stars — Fast growth and high market share

Cash cows — Low growth rate but high share

Dogs — Low growth rate and low market share.

Problem Children or **Question Marks** — Low share but high rate of market growth.

The question is do you join in enthusiastically or launch an attack? Either is possible. If you want to join in, talk earnestly about the strategy for each SBU or brand: build, hold, harvest or divest. Hit back by using the **diffusion curve** to interrogate colleagues about the product life-cycle stage.

If you want to attack then the best route is to question the principle of diversification which underlies this and other similar portfolio strategies. Suggest that the company "stick to the knitting". Deprecate the mental set that such portfolio analysis produces. Refer to Peters and Waterman's analysis of their 'excellent companies'. They didn't think much of diversification and the **Boston Matrix.** It wasn't their consulting group who invented it.

The Boston Group Matrix:

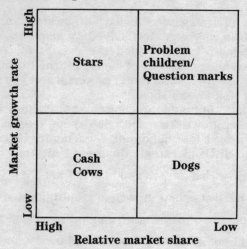

If someone else is attacking the idea of portfolio analysis you remind them that ICI used a similar approach to earn a "better billion". Suggest that you too see merit in earning a "better" million or a "better" £2.99. Nobody can argue with you, but nobody. Then point out that this is a *strategic* issue and what's good enough for ICI should do pretty well for most of the rest of us.

If it's a question of products or brands, tread more cautiously. If you're an academic or a strategist then you should support portfolio planning wholeheartedly (though don't forget to express belief in the power of your brands). Only if you're an out and out action man or street trader can you afford to differ. Even then you're probably better off denying all specialised knowledge and saying the same things in the most down to earth vocabulary you can find.

The Emergency Matrix

There are certain times when the requirement for a marketing plan hits your office like a thunderbolt from Zeus. It might, for example, be an unannounced visit from the Vice-President North-East Regional Co-ordinator for Western Europe, who never gets chart-lagged and positively loves comparing your advertising campaign to that of the Venezuelan company.

In this situation you can:

1. Repeat the last marketing plan and hope he doesn't notice (risky, to say the least).
2. Get the agency to do a new one (comes to the same thing as 1).
3. Use this special emergency matrix for marketing planning.

Across the top are the key elements of the marketing mix; down the side an exhaustive list of verbs covering what you can do about each element of the marketing mix.

Strategy   Marketing mix

	Product	Price	Promotion	Place	Positioning	Packaging
innovate						
imitate						
adopt						
adapt						
ignore						
hold						
improve						
enter						
harvest						
exit						

Take a number of copies of the matrix, prepared for overhead projection, into your meeting along with a selection of different colour OHP pens.

Announce to the group that as the brand-planning process is a continuous cycle, you would like to lead a brainstorming where each strategy is rated out of ten for effectiveness in regard to each element of the mix. Comparisons with Venezuela are the subject of another acetate, of course, and should be encouraged.

After about five minutes of your presentation, everybody should start arguing — led by the Vice President. Sit back with your spare matrix and mark it up according to the direction of the meeting. After about 45 minutes, announce that you'd like to summarise the discussion thus far and to examine the chosen strategies in more detail.

Present the chart and a series of agreed next steps and then sit down. With a bit of luck you will have saved yourself — and the agency — a week's work. Note: this only works once.

Marketing Economics

It is essential to be familiar with the financial jargon you will come across in marketing plans and budgets. The most important are:

Sales volume — Your brand's sales in units: could be gallons, cases, barrels, boxes or lbs.

Sterling sales at RSP — What your brand actually turned over.

Net Sales Volume (NSV) — What your company actually received, less discounts.

Gross contribution — NSV less the 'variable costs'.

34

Net contribution — Gross contribution less 'fixed costs': e.g. heating, lighting, the rental of the corporate HQ and the Chairman's yacht.

Contribution after marketing — What your brand actually puts into the corporate pot.

Breakeven point — Where NSV equals variable plus fixed costs. From here on in you're into profit.

Profit Margin — usually $\dfrac{\text{PBIT}}{\text{sales}}$ or $\dfrac{\text{PBIT}}{\text{NSV}}$ expressed as a %.

2. Commission Market Research

Marketing is an information technology and you can't market blind. Well you *can*, and most marketeers do so from time to time, but in order to do without market research you need to know a little about it.

Because marketing is consumption orientated, the process of meeting needs has been likened to the motion of a boomerang. The return trip happens to be the wedge of research data that whacks you on the head after asking simple questions about what the consumer wants. So beware of asking *simple* questions.

Market research is the petrol of marketing: it's expensive, damaging to the environment and will only take you so far. This has not prevented it from becoming one of the Britain's boom industries. There are of course many different types of market research and the field is characterised by a high degree of semi-masonic jargon designed to put off the lay marketing person.

Do not be put off. The best strategy is always to deploy common sense to penetrate the cloud of un-meaning which tends to hover over most research proposals.

The basic types of market research you should know about are as follows:

Quantitative

(Latin 'quanto' meaning by how much?) This usually involves counting observations amongst large samples of people and is usually expressed via percentages. A typical quantitative finding might be:
'17 per cent of housewives like stuffing'.

Qualitative

(Latin 'qualis' meaning of what kind, sort or nature?) This method seeks not to measure rigorously but rather to 'explore' attitudes and motivations in depth among small samples of people. A typical finding might be:
'stuffing users are inward looking social adventurers'.

Until recently, quantitative researchers have been the underdogs, beavering away in obscurity. Their reports were often telling but irredeemably tedious except for those whose natural diet is numerical. By contrast, qualitative researchers have enjoyed the limelight with sexy research techniques that involved video cameras and bottles of wine and provided lots of good stories about housewives in Chingford and the social mores of C2s.

There are (or were) two main reasons for this ascendancy. Firstly their style. As a group qualitative researchers tend to be personable, intelligent, fluent talkers and very good listeners. They therefore find it easy to bluff their way in marketing. Remember this. You are buying the interpretative (and marketing) skills of one or two people. If they are good hang on to them — if not discard them ruthlessly, regardless of the quality of their presentations. You'll often find an inverse relationship

— the more glossy the report, the more hackneyed the thinking.

Secondly, their viewpoint. Qualitative research at its best is about tomorrow. It's thought-provoking, relevant and extremely difficult to disprove.

By contrast, quantitative research has traditionally been about yesterday. What did people do yesterday (or last month or last year)? But that's changing fast. Quantitative research is hitting back and anyone confident with micro-computers can now score heavily. Be reassured — you don't need to know anything about the techniques or the technology. What you do need is a few useful concepts.

The best is the idea of **modelling,** putting together a computer 'model' of how a particular group of people behave. Once the model is set up you can ask endless 'what if..?' questions.

Another useful computer application is ultra-fine **targetting** for direct selling of any form. New technology and nifty software enables you to locate not just the towns and districts in which your target market is likely to live but also the individual streets.

Continuous surveys are the major studies clients buy on a regular basis in order to measure markets, retailer purchases, consumer sales and changes in consumer attitudes.

Retail audit presentations are usually good for a slanging match between sales and marketing. This is because the figures are always believed to be too low by one side and too high by the other side. Try for a ringside seat but avoid being caught in the clinches.

Consumer panels allow you to explore consumer dynamics. You do not need to know what this means — only that it's what panels are good for.

Tracking studies are used to beat advertising agencies over the head when they reveal a pathetic unprompted awareness score for your product. (Unprompted awareness is what sorts out the real winners — it's all too easy to tell a researcher you've heard of a name on a card. After all you don't want to sound like someone who spends the commercial breaks making cups of tea.)

Ad hoc is the term used to describe any survey conducted to meet specific research objectives on a marketing problem not covered in continuous surveys.

Ad hoc research can be quantitative or qualitative, premium or bargain basement. When you think about commissioning an ad hoc survey consider this:

"If you need it you can't use it" and "if you can use it you don't need it".

The development of this rule is as follows:

'The usefulness of any research is not measured by its inherent quality but by the ability of those on the receiving end to do something about it'.

In-house researchers

Always treat your in-house researchers with a mixture of caution and respect because:

a) Unlike outside market researchers you don't pay their wages (at least not usually). This means that they are not as subservient as they might otherwise be.

b) Market researchers can get very uppity about research, especially when you flout its findings (i.e. *their* findings).

c) Market researchers can help you cut through the waffle, buy effectively and make the results comprehensible.

On balance, it is always worth keeping researchers on your side, encouraging them to take up a 'planning stance' on your brand. This will go down very well.

Market Research Jargon

Acorn: A Classification of Residential Neighbourhoods — Who lives where.

AGB: Audits of Great Britain — Research agency obsessed with looking at the rubbish in people's dustbins. All of us, one day, will be on an AGB panel.

TGI: Target Group Index — Survey much loved by the media to demonstrate that their organ is read by more blue cheese dressing users than anyone else.

TAT: Thematic Apperception Test — Getting consumers to describe their feelings with crayons and pieces of paper.

CATI: Computer Assisted Telephone Interviewing — Resting place for out of work actors to practise their inter-personal communication skills via the London telephone directory.

EPOS: Electronic point of sale — Bar coding.

EFTPOS: Electronic Funds Transfer at Point of Sale — Talk about whether the cashless society is a reality.

IMPOS: Impossible — The consequences of EPOS/EFTPOS on those who have to analyse the data.

STM: Simulated Test Market — Fashionable method of testing the marketing mix.

DAR: Day After Recall — Advertising testing technique on which to pour scorn, unless employed by Procter & Gamble.

CUT: Consumer Usage Test also known as **CLT: Central Location Test** — The opposite of a home placement test.

BLT: Bacon, lettuce and tomato sandwich — Useful to have around at CLTs.

DPP — a) Director of Public Prosecutions. New supervisory body for insider marketing activities; b) Direct Product Profitability. What the trade uses to beat your margins down. Also known as Pandora's Cube.

ECG: Extended Creativity Groups — Expensive and entertaining afternoons with consumers and plenty of TATs.

ABC1C2DE — Social grade. Also known as **SEGs (Socio-Economic Groupings).** A's are judges and generals, B's are marketing men (except Directors), C1's inspect your tax returns, C2's install your central heating, D's remove your rubbish and E's are elderly parents and spendthrift youth at university.

NRS: National Readership Survey — Major study of press readership. How many papers did you look at yesterday?

OTS: Opportunities to see — Average number of times the target audience is supposed see your advertisement.

OTT: Over the top — Usual cost of generating sufficient OTS.

3. Launch New Products

It is proverbial amongst marketing people that new products are a company's lifeblood. It is less obvious that marketing men frequently spill blood (their own included) to make new product development happen.

Only 1 in 20 new products succeed, which means that 19 out of 20 new products and their managers fail. As a successful bluffer you will want to make your career, not break it. What follows, therefore, are the success factors for career development via new products.

a) Ideas are not the problem.
Getting ideas is not the issue these days. You'll find ideas at exhibitions, during the essential yearly trips to Japan or simply by looking at your competitors' catalogues. You can even spend very pleasant awaydays with the Agency brainstorming new concepts.

The real problem you have to address is finding the *right* ideas. In the 1970s many companies fled lemming-like into 'kettle technology' (a.k.a. pot snacks). Huge investment in plant and technology followed, the market proved to be a pot of worms and the inevitable shakedown resulted. Home computers and games software was a similar story.

As a general rule, then, avoid fashion markets. By the time they start generating interest in the press, it's too late for you to do anything useful apart from knocking the idea on the head.

b) Know what the company is actually good at.
Not many companies are able to change their characteristics overnight. You will therefore stand a much better chance of picking a project with potential if you understand the assets and liabilities of your company.

A key concept to raise when your Managing Director

discusses diversification is the idea of 'the experience curve barrier to entry'. This means that if you've never ridden a bicycle before, the chances are that you'll end up sitting on the floor looking foolish.

c) Get a product champion.
Academic research has revealed the importance of a product champion to new product success. This excludes your spouse, your mother and your Agency Account Director.

The product champion is a very senior company executive who believes in your project and can help you cut through the politics and get decisions taken. Great care, however, should be taken when the project champion happens to be the MD and the product is his pet project.

d) Do not underestimate the workload.
Setting up a new business is extremely time-consuming. When a product has no history everybody in the organisation has to be educated about it. Given the lead-times involved in capital expenditure, plant, trials, packaging and advertising, it is sensible to have plenty of help on hand. If this is not available in-house, use an Agency to do the legwork.

e) Decide a clear role for market research.
Full rigour product development consists of lots of market research stages. Any or all of the following could be used:

- early 'exploratory' qualitative research
- concept research in groups
- home placement or hall test surveys
- advertising development research
- packaging research
- test marketing (e.g, STM)

When commissioning research and spending the company's money decide what your motivations are. Do you want to:

1. Blow the project out of the water?
2. Get the product to market by hook or by crook?
3. Satisfy a spirit of enquiry?

f) Sell it to the salesforce.

The hardest test of any new product and by far the trickiest hurdle to negotiate is the response of the salesforce. Since they have such an unpleasant job being nice to buyers who are not nice to them they enjoy the role reversal. You are selling, they are buying and they make it difficult.

Do not put your faith in lasers and pretty slides: put yourself in their shoes. It's a wet Monday morning and you are sitting in a bleak reception with 27 other salesmen drinking undrinkable coffee. Now what are the real benefits of the product?

g) Watch the first few days of the launch carefully.

Just as the television pollsters can predict the winner's majority in the General Election from the first few declarations, so you can judge whether this project is your responsibility or someone else's from:

- the results of the first trade presentations.
- consumer purchasing rates and repeat buying from panel data and adhoc surveys.

Post launch research can be highly useful but there is a delicate balance to be struck between saving your own skin or finding out how you can do better next time.

Note: whilst large NPD successes are the products of many fathers, you will rarely meet a marketing man who has launched a failure.

h) Avoid the effects of failure.

- Deny the failure entirely ('we achieved 75 per cent sterling distribution in the North-East').
- Blame Production (or Sales) for crimes unspecified.
- Blame the retailers for bringing out an own label six weeks after launch. (Always a good one — particularly if it's true.)
- Blame the company for failing to realise the necessity of serious media spending.
- Philosophize on the problems (and costs) of creating a 'real' brand these days.
- Vigorously affirm the importance of taking big risks for big rewards. A host of 'me-toos' doesn't help anybody very much.
- Stress the problems inherent in 'discontinuous innovations' (i.e. *really* new ideas). The implication is that you have had the courage to think big and bet big.
- Cite other new product failures (the Sinclair C5, the Ford Edsel, new smoking materials, TVP food products). On second thoughts, don't.
- Find another job before anyone has noticed what's happened.

New Product Jargon

Added value — What most new products claim to have. Generic claim in sales presentations and sales presenters. Excuse for a high price.

Blind Test — A consumer test without identifying the product.

Concept/Product Fit — Getting it right. Harder than it looks.

Existing Products (OPD) — Making the most of existing brand assets e.g. stretching the brand name into new territories. Now a whole new field of NPD.

Insulation — The attempt to provide barriers to competitive entry into the market targeted by your new product.

Kill point — Termination at the worst possible moment. Ensure that your employment is not similarly affected.

Me-too — Competitive entrant in your new market.

Me-too late — What you would never be guilty of launching.

Minivan — Not your company car but a clever kind of test market.

Monadic — Testing your product by itself rather than against other products.

No Go — Try again.

Roll-out — The extension of a product out of its test market area. Not to be confused with roll up.

STM — Trendy kind of test market. Expensive, but liked by Marketing Directors.

4. Brand Things

What is branding?

The process of communicating with the customer is the bit most marketeers enjoy the most; developing their skill and talent in the serious art of **branding**.

There is a world of difference between a product and a brand; between Ribes Nigrum and Ribena; between ordinary denims and Levi 501s; between catfood and Whiskas. Products are generic; brands are unique.

Classical branding is a semi-religious activity requiring much respect for and worshipping of the brand values which have been created and reinforced over time.

Brand values are a mixture of functional factors like price, performance and, say, taste and the emotional values connoted by the brand name, the style of its advertising and the properties of the package: the Oxo Mum.

The reason why marketeers take branding so seriously is that branding is about *the security of future profits*. It is relatively easy to get a single sale, it is far more efficient to create a pattern of loyalty somewhat resembling inertia selling. It is much easier to defend a brand which has far more dimensions to differentiate it than a commodity. Smash and its Martians were far more defensible than Cadbury Instant Mash Potato.

Branding brings other benefits too. Having created a distinctive image with the consumers, brands can be extended within their area of authority. St Ivel's brand 'Shape' has the proposition 'Half the fat, all the taste' and whilst currently the range is made up of dairy products, 'Shape' could in time travel to other product fields where its brand values are relevant, e.g. low fat ready meals.

Where brands are extended beyond their 'franchise', or where brand values are diluted by inconsistent advertising messages or investment, brands can easily lay themselves open to attack from other manufacturer brands, or even, in the case of FMPG, the retailer's own brand, which in these days of retailer marketing and power, are some of the most powerful around.

Bluffers should treat retailer brands with care.

Positioning

If brand values are the sum total of the physical and psychological attributes of a product, **positioning** is the word for how that brand is focused against the marketplace and its competitors. Good bluffers will display elegant positioning thinking. For example:

★ The Listening Bank
★ The Action Bank
★ The Thoroughbred Bank
★ The Bank that Likes to Say Yes

You will observe that whilst banks are all very similar in what they do, their positionings play to different styles of doing business. The best positioning is that which is both consistent with brand values *and* most effectively touches the consumer's nerve.

Products in different markets can have differing positionings, though many global marketeers seek to avoid this. As markets evolve or change in nature, a product can be *repositioned* (see Product Life-Cycle). Lucozade moved from the bedside drink for invalids to a highly distinctive 'adult' soft drink.

Most marketeers will run into positioning issues at some time. So here is a positioning checklist to get you off to an impressive start. Simply check the relevance of each idea as a platform for your brand.

Prestige, Fun, Health, Excitement, Mystery, Romance, Style, Sophistication, Convenience, Quality, Fashion, Tradition, Bargain, Family, Individual, Contemporary.

But beware of 'positioning' statements that are merely meaningless straplines. 'Tomorrow's finest food today', for example, says nothing. Over use in the marketing mill has robbed the words of all meaning.

5. Make Presentations

Whatever their personal style all successful presenters are consummate bluffers. The whole art of successful presentation is bluff. Expensive courses on presentation put it slightly differently, but that's what they mean.

Firstly, the content. This is the least important bit. It's not what you say but how you say it. Go for short, pithy generalisations — a few words to each slide or chart. Intersperse these with heavyweight numbers charts which you pass over arrogantly as an *example* of the work *you* have done. Then turn rapidly to the three bullet point summary. Consider providing a back-up Databook which will remain an unread and reassuring presence after the meeting.

Expend your effort on commanding your audience. David Ogilvy always recommended reading every word on the chart exactly as it was written. He believed, probably rightly, that most of the audience were rarely awake enough to cope with two different messages coming at them. You acknowledge the truth of his remark but flatter *this* audience by crediting them with the capacity to be able to read and listen at the same time. They can't, but it should help to confuse them.

Insist that the presentation is rehearsed — with *all the material* that you'll use. Otherwise Murphy's Law will undoubtedly strike. This is crucial — there's no point in unnecessarily putting yourself in situations where you have to bluff to stay alive.

And, most important of all, get the provisions right. Never produce what's expected. Whether you're in the champagne and caviar or tea and biscuits category, make it one level better or one level worse than your audience expects. Then make up for office coffee by expensive biscuits.

6. Buy Advertising

Agency People

Receptionist — Easily the most powerful person in the Agency. Probably knows more about your account than the Account Director.

Chairman — Interesting cross-breed of public school housemaster and the Invisible Man.

Managing Director — The Agency boss. Usually features in meetings when the Agency has something to gain or to lose. Asking for his comments on the latest Nielsen should stop him in his tracks.

Creative Director — High earner, high profile and high style. Usually into Zen, the SDP or his third wife.

Account Director — Living proof that opposites attract. Probably a defrocked marketeer. Treat with a mixture of suspicion and sympathy.

Account Planner — Smart-arse account man who turns your brief into baby talk for the creative department. Watch out when they feel a matrix coming on.

Account Manager — Usually a nice person who gets it in the neck from everybody. Still, this is advertising and it is *your* money.

Creative Teams — The group whose function it is to create, and they do so frequently, but not necessarily advertisements. Watch them turn your product into gold and silver — usually D & AD Awards.

Traffic — The liquid engineering which keeps the creative department running smoothly.

Media Planners — Often second class citizens in Agencies who compensate by engrossing themselves in TVRs,

OTS, frequency schedules and response functions. By far the nicest crowd to have a drink with and you get invited to places like the Bahamas for conferences about 'Whither Television?'.

Media Buyers — The ones who buy time from TV contractors and play a demon mixture of poker and chess. They can save you (or lose you) a lot of money. Do not be fooled by the accent or the beer consumption.

Pitching Etiquette

One of the most curious rituals of advertising is the elaborate courtship behaviour which develops between you, the client, and Agencies seeking your business.

As an advanced bluffer, you will realise the necessity of observing certain customs and practices when you ask Agencies to present their credentials. (The word comes from the latin, credo, meaning 'I believe'. Cynics might say 'incredentials' is a more accurate description.)

a) Do not laugh spontaneously and out loud as the Agency presents its philosophy or says it doesn't have one. Agencies take philosophy very seriously and hours of client time are expended developing such classics as: 'We prefer to work in partnership with our clients' or 'We offer unique total communications solutions'.

b) It is accepted behaviour to show neutral body language in the course of the presentation, revealing neither interest nor boredom. An occasional note on the agency pad with the agency pen is a good ploy. This is a good time to compile your action list for the morrow.

c) When the case histories have finished, pass no judgement, give no praise, say "Thank you for that" and ask them a really heavy duty marketing question like: "How many parking spaces for clients do you have?"

d) Then ask them a vaguely relevant question like: "Do you think brands *can* recapture share from private label?" After about 20 minutes of live brainstorming by the Agency say: "Thank you, that was useful."

e) To close the meeting, ask to meet the people who would actually work on the account. Then pick up whatever goodies are available and leave. Remember this is your moment of greatest power. It's downhill all the way from here.

High Noon at the Agency

Once you have correctly played the mating game, you have to get down to the mundane task of getting the advertising out of the Agency. Getting your advertising is not as easy as it seems. You may be absolutely certain that this is what will happen:

1. You will discover that the campaign your Managing Director liked 'bombs' in research and there are just six weeks to the Sales Conference and twelve weeks to the national launch.

2. You will uncover an omission in the section of the Agency's presentation dealing with the leadtime for commercials.

3. You will receive a document from the planner entitled 'First Thoughts on an Approach to the Creative Brief'.

None of this is reassuring. Nor is the Account Director's quip that Beethoven's Ninth was not written overnight. Resist the temptation to point out that Mozart usually wrote a symphony before breakfast. It will get a good laugh but no action. Good bluffers know that shock tactics are required. Arrange a meeting between you, the MD or Marketing Director and the Agency boss. Energise the whole Agency by threatening:

51

a) Not to sign the Agency's contract
b) Not to commit to media expenditure
c) To use a creative hotshop to do the work
d) To get a media independent to buy the media at reduced rates of commission.
e) To ring up *Campaign*.

This will get you your ads, but the next question is what do they mean when they are presented to you?

Breaking Agency Codes

What They Say	*What They Mean*
Strategically sound	Boring ad
Well branded	Very boring ad
An idea so simple...	Extremely boring ad
The product as hero is old hat	We think the product's crap
We think X (a noted personality) says so much about the brand	The product really *is* crap
It blew their minds in research	Consumers think the product's crap
The product's very distinctive	It's outrageous
It's highly campaignable	We can make even **more** on production
It'll *work* in the press	They can't afford television
It's ideal for television	There's a big budget here
We've done a 60 second and a 30 second version	Bet the nurd will go for the 30
Make 2 for the price of 1	Make 1 for the price of 2
Look how we really built on your existing property	But we had to level it first
Imagine the trade ad	We hope you can because we can't
The Agency view is...	We don't agree

7. Promote Sales

They also serve who sales promote. Good Sales Promotions Agencies can make your money work extremely hard. They are more effective at gaining trial, generating sales and creating product loyalty than any of the other Agencies you may choose to use.

Original ideas are a help — so long as they don't land you in court for infringing one or more of the many laws that govern sales promotions in general. Good ideas, old and new, are probably a better bet. Nobody ever won national recognition through their innovative sales promotions.

Good ideas are those which cost little, are easy to manage, keep the retailers sweet and meet your objectives.

Be clear in your own mind what exactly you want to do. Against the consumer you may wish to:

- Gain trial
- Grab short term volume
- Switch to larger packs
- Reward loyal users

Against the retailer the major objectives are to:

- Get more stock in
- Nobble the competition
- Get trial
- Encourage staff awareness of your product

Finally, there are the million and one incentive schemes to ginger up your sales force.

Sales promotions are about noise — creating it and cutting through it. Remember that there's a sort of Hawthorne Effect: it doesn't matter what you do as long as you keep changing things. In a series of experiments in America in the 1930s, the said Hawthorne, an industrial psychologist, discovered that brighter lights and louder music pushed up production-line productivity. He also discovered that lower lights and quieter music had exactly the same effect. The change was what mattered. It made people feel they were being looked after, that an effort was being made on their behalf. This, by the way, includes your bosses.

Promotion Jargon

Banded offers — The promotional equivalent of the blind date.

BOGOF — Not necessarily an insult: Buy One and Get One Free.

Competitions — The lifeblood of sales promotions. Watch out for the heavy hand of the law if there's not at least some element of skill.

Extra product — 33% more. Unfortunately at least 33% of the population don't understand just what that percentage increase *means*.

Collector devices — Blackmail to buy more.

Collaborative cross-product offers — Two manufacturers in bed together.

Price reductions — Short-term sales boost at the expense of your brand personality and image.

Shelf talkers — How to maximise every square inch of promotional space.

SLPs: Self Liquidating Promotions — The art of getting your promotions for free — courtesy of manufacturer discount and the punter's contribution.

Wobblers — Store decoration at your expense.

8. Exploit PR

Like Sales Promotions operations, PR Agencies can be divided into those with good ideas and those with no ideas at all. Good PR can cost very little, bad PR can cost you and your brand a fortune. The trick is to pick the right one.

PR Agencies come in a variety of shapes and sizes. Those who boast of their 'strategic' thinking will want to explain your own marketing plan to you. Those who offer 'total communications solutions' want to do your advertising as well.

To get the most out of your Agency you should:

1. Make sure the Agency puts both an ideas person and an organiser on your team. Plenty of Agencies bubble over with bright ideas, but can't deliver on time, to specification or within budget. Others can manage the nuts and bolts but can't write, have no imagination and no contacts.
2. Ask for proof of the effectiveness of the campaign. PR Agencies have worked so long and so hard to convince a properly sceptical public of their ability to provide measurable results that they can't deny you this request. Whether you allow yourself to be persuaded is up to you.
3. Get them to define and target each of the audiences you're interested in. If you want to communicate with the managers of major pension funds, daily column inches in the *Sun* won't do you much good.
4. Make sure they take every opportunity to get someone else to fund *your* PR: a Building Society for that campaign on home security; a major brewer to promote your new book on Alehouses of the World. And so on.

9. Call in Consultancies

There are consultancies to deal with most problems and marketing is no exception. Marketing consultancies come in many shapes and sizes.

The Ad Agency as Consultancy

Advertising Agencies are increasingly laying claim to marketing expertise — as a bolt on to their more profitable services. Keep in mind that there are two problems with such expertise.

1. The commission structure of Advertising Agencies does not sit well with the largely fee-based consultancy approach. To match usual levels of profitability within the Agency thay have to charge high fees relative to the service they can provide. Alternatively they are used to bring in advertising business — see 2. below.
2. Advertising Agencies have only one solution to most business problems: advertising. This is often neither appropriate nor financially feasible.

The Big Boys

Large Management Consultancies such as Boston Consulting Group, Bain & Co. and McKinsey's will undoubtedly undertake marketing problems. Apart from the clout that any recommendations will undoubtedly carry, there are three things to note:

1. You may get the full rigour solution involving complete financial and organisational restructuring.
2. International consultancies tend to relocate their employees at the drop of a hat. You may never see the same principal twice.
3. The work is usually done by extremely bright graduates with no experience of the real world, *your* world. It depends whether you like bright young graduates.

It goes without saying that these operations are expensive beyond the dreams of avarice.

The Rest

A ragbag of companies and individuals. You should expect service beyond the call of duty, creativity under fire, an ability to meet deadlines (whatever happens), and a certain capacity to think intelligently. Many people believe that the last is the least important.

You have to rely on past experience and contacts and on personal recommendations from those who wish you well. Beware both those with too few clients and those with too many. Remember that, as with Market Research Agencies, you're buying the skills of one or more individuals. Make sure that those individuals actually do *your* work and keep your antennae tuned for fellow bluffers.

JARGON

Jargon is the lifeblood of the marketeer and a little will take you a long way. This, of course, is in the best tradition of marketing.

Above the line — What marketeers are persuaded to spend by their advertising agency (the unspeakable in full pursuit of the award).

Achilles Heel — The company's key weakness.

Below the line — What people other than advertising agencies persuade you to spend on your brands.

Awaydays — In theory, intensive think tank sessions. In practice a chance to wear casual clothes and to spend a pleasant day with the Agency at a hotel somewhere round the M25. Judge Agencies by the quality of their awaydays.

Brainstorming — A method of generating ideas. Associated with awaydays. Always good for a laugh.

Bundling — Obscure Scandinavian custom of wrapping hot-blooded adolescents of opposite sex up in blankets — round *and* between them. Presumably to excite desire whilst hindering performance. Marketing men do the same thing — putting two products together to persuade the gullible public they're getting a better deal.

Cannibalisation — Getting sales on one product by taking them from another of your own brands, rather than one of the competition's.

Culture — Trendy term to explain how things are done in a company. Often used as a reason why something can't be done: as in 'It goes against the grain of the culture here'.

Cutting edge — A good thing to have in a marketing plan. Strategic planners use **Differential Advantage** instead.

Demarketing — What marketeers often do by accident, occasionally by intent: take action that decreases rather than increases their sales.

Diversification — The most effective commercial way of boosting egos and losing shareholders' money.

Economies of scale — Justification for some very grand plans.

Elasticity of demand — What you hope for when you reduce the price. If you're right the increased volume more than compensates for the lost revenue per unit.

FMCG — Fast moving consumer goods, e.g. confectionery, toiletries, groceries. Good for baffling non-marketing colleagues. **FMPG** is a variant. P stands for 'packaged'.

Four P's — The four essentials of the marketing mix: product, price, place and promotion. You can't ignore them so don't bother to try.

Gap analysis — What you have to do to spot the gaps in the market.

Grow, harvest, exit — The only busines strategies you need: growth is good for headlines in the marketing press and getting the next job; exit is good for headlines; harvest is no good for anything — except funding growth.

Inertia selling — The process by which business book clubs make more money out of you than you do out of them.

Key success factors — The keys to fame and fortune in any given market. Always worth asking somebody else before they ask you.

KVI — Known Value Item. Change the price with care and at your peril.

Lifestyle — What the Agency has and you would like.

Line extension — The kneejerk response to NPD assignments. Just beware of adding so many variants to your existing brand that you destroy the image and **cannibalise** your own sales.

Marketing mixes — What results when brand managers put all the marketing ingredients together and give them a good shaking. The best mixes look good (at least on paper), taste nice, cost a lot and do a lot of damage. The acid test is who gets damaged — you or the competition?

Matrix — The lego brick of marketing thinking. Do not confuse with Dot Matrix, whoever she is.

Parameter — The limit, as in 'Our budget parameters don't go that far'.

Projective techniques — The researcher's prerogative. Silly answers to silly questions at silly prices.

Scenario — The non-controversial way of breaking bad news to the Managing Director, as in 'The current scenario calls for a high degree of risk management'.

Share of voice — Percentage of your advertising spend relative to your competitors. The subtle question is what **share of mind** is your advertising achieving.

Spontaneous awareness — What your boss never shows when you come up with a good idea.

SWOT — Strengths, weaknesses, opportunities, threats analysis in market planning. Also known as sweat analysis for obvious reasons.

Synectics — Posh word for brainstorm.

Synergy — The excuse for a number of grandiose management follies.

Test marketing — Prohibitively expensive and very public way of demonstrating how well you've organised a new product launch.

The Three R's — The Product Manager's Life-Cycle: Repackage, Relaunch and Resign.

THE AUTHORS

Graham Harding started life in rural Essex before grabbing a few glittering prizes in Cambridge. His inability to read medieval Latin and a vague desire to do something useful ended thoughts of academic life. He therefore launched himself on the jobs market as a publisher and spent several happy years learning about the less sophisticated side of marketing.

Repositioning as a fully-fledged marketing man was the logical next step. A period of line extension and a desire for higher penetration took him to The Value Engineers, a small and highly individual Marketing Consultancy.

The Bluffer's Guide to Marketing is his first venture into print under his own name. The other names were much more prestigious but he is not at liberty to reveal them. His ambition is to write a book that will make real money.

Paul Walton was conceived in Walsall, test marketed at Brasenose College, Oxford, and launched at a Paddington advertising agency.

His first products included Swedish cars, German lager and British Intelligence. Assigned to a food account he early distinguished himself in new product development by recommending that the clients' starch-reduced rolls should be relaunched as loft insulation materials.

After ten years of developing products for other people, and after a major awayday with himself, he finally launched his own product: The Value Engineers. A keen student of history, his *Mastermind* specialist subject would be; 'The Cooking Sauce Market — 1974 to the present day'.

THE BLUFFER'S GUIDES

Available now @ £1.00 each:

Accountancy	Management
Antiques	Marketing
Bluffing	Music
Class	Paris
Computers	Philosophy
Consultancy	Photography
Feminism	Publishing
Golf	Sex
Hi-Fi	Teaching
Hollywood	Television
Jazz	Theatre
Literature	Wine

Coming March 1988:

Ballet
Cricket
Maths

All these books are available at your local bookshop or newsagent, or can be ordered direct from the publisher. Just tick the titles you require and fill in the form below. Prices and availability subject to change without notice.

Ravette Limited, 3 Glenside Estate, Star Road, Partridge Green, Horsham, West Sussex RH13 8RA

Please send a cheque or postal order, and allow the following for postage and packing. UK 25p for one book and 10p for each additional book ordered.

Name..

Address..

....

THE BLUFFER'S GUIDES

In preparation:

Advertising
Architecture
Astrology
Bank Managers
Beliefs
The Body
Cinema
The Classics
Defence
Espionage
Finance
Gambling
High Society
Journalism
Law
Millionaires
Modern Art
Opera
Politics
Property
Psychiatry

Public Relations
Secret Societies
Selling
Ski-ing
Stocks & Shares
Travel
University
World Affairs

The Americans
The Australians
The British
The French
The Germans
The Japanese

Amsterdam
Berlin
Hong Kong
Moscow
New York

"At dawn the river seems a shade—
A liquid shadow deep as space;
But when the sun the mist has laid,
A diamond shower smites its face."

—*John Burroughs*

WILDSAM PURSUITS

Places are endlessly complex: time, geography, culture and happenings layered with millions of stories. And often, one realizes that a place carries a specific heritage, a definitive pursuit that people build their lives around, a common trade or precious resource that might set the course for generations.

For the Hudson Valley & Catskills, this pursuit is art and antiques.

Our deepest thanks to all the contributors, writers, friends and
other generous locals who offered their insight and wisdom,
including Pippa Biddle and Ben Davidson [who wrote and
researched while expecting their first baby], the well-traveled
Tracey Minkin [we went full circle], the great connector Jeff
Gordinier, Ernesto Roman of the Deer Mountain Inn, and our
essayists Ruth Reichl and Sandy Allen for beautiful stories of life
on either side of the river. Renaissance man Steven Weinberg,
thank you for these joyful illustrations. And of course, endless
gratitude to the Wildsam crew, especially Becca Worby and
Jared Briere, for helping paint this portrait.

WILDSAM FIELD GUIDES™

Published in the United States
by Wildsam Field Guides, Austin, Texas.

ISBN 978-1-4671-9948-3

Illustrations by Steven Weinberg

To find more field guides, please visit
www.wildsam.com

CONTENTS

Discover the people and places
that tell the story of the Hudson Valley & Catskills

WELCOME

——

FROM A ROSE-COLORED ranch house off the rivulet roads lacing the Catskill foothills, The Band etched an opening line into the American music canon: "I pulled into Nazareth / Was feelin' about half past dead." "The Weight" is just one of the epochal songs on the album *Music From Big Pink*, the title referring to the nickname for their West Saugerties home where they also wrote dozens of songs with then-Woodstock resident Bob Dylan. But their best renditions of his work didn't come from Pink's fabled basement; it was at nearby Bearsville Studio they recorded "When I Paint My Masterpiece," a mandolin-stippled antiquary journey.

Dylan once told a journalist the song was about "someplace you'd like to be beyond your experience. Something that is so supreme and first rate that you could never come back down from the mountain." It's easy to hear shades of the painter Thomas Cole there. Cole spent his short life trying to mirror the captivating majesty of the epic landscapes before him, inventing the country's first collective art movement, the Hudson River School, in the process. "If the imagination is shackled, and nothing is described but what we see, seldom will anything truly great be produced either in painting or poetry," he said.

Revolutionary First Lady Eleanor Roosevelt, who grew up—not far from Cole's studio—in Hyde Park, described a Hudson Valley sunset in August 1944. She wrote, "The path of gold upon the river stretched straight across from bank to bank, and the clouds were tinged with soft colors. ... I could almost wish that God had not given weak human beings quite so much freedom, for we make of his beautiful world such a sorry place at times." Roosevelt's premonition officially came to pass in 1984, when the EPA declared the Hudson River one of the country's most polluted sites. And since then, problems with privatized land barring access to the Hudson's shores, cresting property values in the region and an unprecedented swell of newcomers have all complicated the picture.

But if there is a sign seen in the new generation of young farmers and artists from every background planting seeds of progress into this hallowed ground, reflecting new and untold stories in their work, it is this: There is still inspiration here to reflect a place they want to be. There is always another masterpiece to paint. —The Editors

ESSENTIALS

Trusted intel and travel info about iconic culture, geography
and entry points to the traditions and landscapes of the
Hudson Valley & Catskills

PLANNING

TRAIN
Amtrak
Empire Service Line
amtrak.com

....

BUS LINE
Trailways
Catskills from Albany/NYC
trailways.com

LANDMARK BRIDGES
RIP VAN WINKLE BRIDGE
Catskill to Hudson
Cantilever tollway weds equally scenic vistas on either side of river.

....

WALKWAY OVER HUDSON
Highland to Poughkeepsie
An 1889 railway turned world's longest raised pedestrian bridge.

MEDIA
MAGAZINE
Chronogram
Multifaceted monthly, part of media company that includes *The River Newsroom.*

....

ARTS & CULTURE JOURNAL
Upstate Diary
Glossy, coffee-table-worthy quarterly.

....

RADIO
WJFF 90.5 FM Radio Catskill
News plus podcasts, from *Borscht Beat* to *Farm and Country.*

CLIMATE
 No matter the month, don't forget to bring a sweater. With cool days deep into summer, it's not hard to see why this corner of the country has long been a refuge for city dwellers—especially the Catskill Mountains where 70s top the typical July highs. Autumn's awe-inspiring foliage is a prelude to frigid winters when snow blankets the landscape, so take care while driving windy back roads. On average, Kingston sees around 40 inches per year, while Catskills towns like Livingston Manor can have close to 70.

CALENDAR
JAN	Storm King Winter Weekends
FEB	Black History Month Kingston
MAR	Seed Song Farm Maple March
APR	Catskills Trout Tales
MAY	Kaatsbaan Spring Festival
JUN	Queer Summer Nights
JUL	Bard Summerscape
AUG	Phoenicia International Festival of the Voice
SEP	Oldtone Roots Music Festival
OCT	Woodstock Film Festival
NOV	Basilica Farm & Flea
DEC	Sinterklaas Festival Day

GEOGRAPHY

Notable terrain formations and where to find them.

KILLS
The Dutch word for a body of water was given by early settlers to many upstate rivers, streams and creeks leading into the Hudson River. *Catskill Creek*

....

CLOVES
Also called gorges, those found in the Catskills were formed by erosive water from receding glaciers. *Platte Clove*

WATERFALLS
Kills carved through stony mountainsides over millennia. Spring snowmelt spurs fresh water down over impressive, sheer drops. *Buttermilk Falls*

....

GLACIAL ERRATICS
Isolated boulders carried by melting glaciers. Another remnant of how ice shaped the area. *Patterson's Pellet*

FJORD
A Scandinavian term for a deep narrow inlet lined by cliffs. The Hudson River is classified as a fjord. *Hudson Highlands State Park Preserve*

....

FORESTS
Glorious color courtesy of thick maple- and oak-dominated stands. Some old-growth still remains. *Lake Mohonk*

TRADITIONS

A heritage of farming, fishing, art and design.

Cider — Apple orchards have deep roots here stretching back to the 1600s. New York State is the leading producer of hard cider. *Left Bank Ciders, Catskill*

Farming — Younger growers carry small-scale steads onward with new sustainable practices. *Montgomery Place Orchards, Red Hook*

Architecture — Centuries of building styles endure and evolve, from Dutch Colonial farmhouses to modernist marvels. *Historic Hudson, Hudson*

Fly Fishing — The sport took root in the United States by way of streams teeming with trout in Catskills. *Willowemoc Creek, Livingston Manor*

Visual Art — Upstate scenery has informed everything from landscape oils to kinetic sculpture. *Art Omi, Ghent*

ANTIQUES DESTINATIONS

A quick guide to noted shops and auction houses.

HOFFMAN'S BARN
Started as pole barn selling produce, now filled with treasures.

PUBLIC SALE AUCTION HOUSE
Themes like "Weird and Wonderful" and "Moderniture."

COXSACKIE ANTIQUE CENTER
On-site reference library and "matchmaker" program.

A. THERIEN
Hyper-curated selection in tiny town of Cairo.

KINGSTON CONSIGNMENTS
Collectibles and coveted finds across all eras.

THE ANTIQUE WAREHOUSE
The largest shop in the Northeast U.S.

ZABORSKI EMPORIUM
Architectural salvage, with doors, stained glass, clawfoots.

STAIR GALLERIES
Live auctions on Hudson's Warren Street twice a month.

NEVEN & NEVEN MODERNE
Midcentury modern focus. McCobb, Nelson, Baughman.

MOONEY'S AUCTION SERVICE
Old-school gavel bangers in a Catskills hamlet.

CULTURAL INSTITUTIONS

THOMAS COLE NATIONAL HISTORIC SITE
218 Spring St, Catskill

The Hudson River School founder's butter-colored home and studio. Hear actor Jamie Bell read the artist's words in *The Parlors* exhibit.

....

DIA:BEACON
3 Beekman St, Beacon

Hudson Valley star of museum "constellation" in 11 locations. Contemporary art pilgrimage site. Work by Andy Warhol, Gerhard Richter, Nancy Holt, etc.

....

ART OMI
1405 Co Rte 22, Ghent

Clouds on ladders, a monolithic grocery list and an epic-sized doe are just a few sights on 120-acre sculpture park. Large indoor gallery also.

SCENIC DRIVES
AND PUBLIC LANDS

Back roads and natural sites across the Hudson Valley and Catskills.

STATE ROUTE 90

A long C-shaped route glides through the most bucolic towns and hamlets of the Catskills for 282 miles. Farmstands, antiques and hiking trails galore. *Kingston to Warren County*

....

TACONIC STATE PARKWAY

A truck-free scenic drive through the Taconic Mountains lets riders experience one of the first pathways to the area, even before cars. *LaGrangeville to Chatham*

....

KAATERSKILL FALLS

A spiritual axis for the Mohican tribe and artistic muse for Thomas Cole, Washington Irving and more. The two-tiered, 260-foot-drop waterfall still bewitches. *Hunter*

....

MINNEWASKA STATE PARK PRESERVE

About a 90-minute drive from NYC. Plant yourself on the sublime Shawangunk Mountain ridge [2,000-ft. elevation]. May through November, pitch a tent at Samuel F. Pryor III Campground, with its community fire pit and bath house. *Ulster County*

....

BEAR MOUNTAIN STATE PARK

Straddles both sides of the Hudson River. A popular spot for bikers and boaters. Also has a rehabilitation zoo for bears, otters, deer, bald eagles and owls. *Rockland and Orange Counties*

....

HUDSON HIGHLANDS STATE PARK PRESERVE

Wilderness with 8,000 acres of undeveloped land and 70 miles of trails, amateur to expert, along the Hudson's estuarine shore. Many a high, rocky summit overlooking the grandeur. *Cold Spring*

....

209 CORRIDOR

Contemplative drive through southwestern Ulster County that covers the intersection of Indigenous to Revolution-era history. Many hamlets on the way. Stop to send a postcard. *Ulster County*

CULTURE

FILM

A Quiet Place

Woodstock: Three Days that Defined a Generation

The Girl on the Train

Dirty Dancing

The Seagull

Martha Marcy May Marlene

The Place Beyond the Pines

Crip Camp

Land of Little Rivers

Our Idiot Brother

Super Troopers

MUSIC

The Band
Music from Big Pink

Bob Dylan
The Basement Tapes

Real Estate
In Mind

Pete Seeger
"My Dirty Stream
[The Hudson River Song]"

The National
Sleep Well Beast

BOOKS

▷ *World's End* by T.C. Boyle: A historical acid trip that layers protagonist Walter Van Brunt's modern-day bender with the stories of his ancestors, the Valley's Indigenous tribes and Dutch settlers, from the 1600s to the 1960s.

▷ *The Blade Between* by Sam J. Miller: A gay photographer reluctantly returns to his hometown of Hudson and, with old friends, tries to rile up residents over local politics. Gets much more than he bargained for.

▷ *Paradise, New York* by Eileen Pollack: Lucy Appelbaum tries to restart her own life by reviving her family's Jewish resort in the Catskills.

▷ *Freedom's Gardener: James F. Brown, Horticulture, and the Hudson Valley in Antebellum America* by Myra B. Young Armstead: How one formerly enslaved man cultivates a new life in the Upstate soil.

▷ *The Hudson Valley: The First 250 Million Years: A Mostly Chronological and Occasionally Personal History* by David Levin: Essay collection covers all ground, from glaciers to revolution to craft beer.

▷ *My Side of the Mountain* by Jean Craighead George: A Newbery Medal-winning, coming-of-age story about a runaway escaping to the Catskills.

ISSUES

Water Pollution	From 1947 to 1977, General Electric dumped more than a million pounds of polychlorinated biphenyls [PCBs] into the Hudson River, leading the EPA to deem 200 miles of it a Superfund site, a name reserved for some of the country's most contaminated land. Clean-up efforts have helped but PCBs remain high in some areas. **EXPERT:** *Dan Shapley, Riverkeeper Inc.*
Affordable Housing	A longstanding issue exacerbated by city dwellers looking for space during the COVID-19 pandemic. Skyrocketing property values are pricing out longtime residents, and waitlists for subsidized units range from 2 to 5 years. **EXPERT:** *Diana Kingsbury, Nobody Leaves Mid-Hudson*
Ticks and Mosquitos	Climate change and land development have widened the window of transmission and travel area of vector-borne diseases transmitted by ticks, mosquitos and fleas. Lyme is on the rise and Zika is expected to increase as tiger mosquitoes spread north. **EXPERT:** *Mary Beth Pfeiffer, investigative writer and author of* Lyme: The First Epidemic of Climate Change
Congestion	A 60 percent increase in visitors to Catskills parks from 2007 to 2017 has led to issues with overcrowding, sanitation and degradation of trails. The Department of Environmental Conservation announced the creation of a strategic planning initiative to address visitor congestion. **EXPERT:** *Ramsay Adams, Catskill Mountainkeeper*

STATISTICS

216 ....Depth in feet of "World's End," Hudson River's deepest point
$358,250 .....Dutchess County's median home price, a 30% increase since 2019
22 ....Percentage Black population in city of Hudson
4,180 .... Height in feet of Slide Mountain, tallest peak in Catskills
18,278,636.............. Number of apple trees in 1875 according to NY census
13.5 .... Height in feet of Gnome Chomsky in Kerhonkson

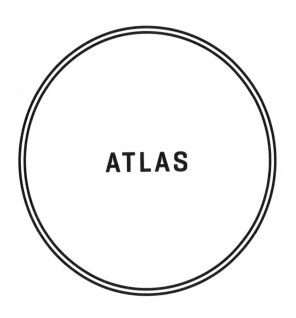

ATLAS

A guide to the lands and places of the Hudson Valley &
Catskills, including curated favorites, communities large and
small, and a road trip up the river and into the mountains

BESTS

FOOD & DRINK

RURAL RESPITE

Phoenicia Diner

5681 Hwy 28
Phoenicia

A mountainside haven with a David Lynch-ian facade. Breakfast standards, yes, but also beef stroganoff, pan-seared trout, cocktails.

....

BAKERY

Breadfolks

322 Warren St
Hudson

Exquisitely scored sourdough loaves, lacquered turnovers, and the foretold-in-legend "cruffins."

....

BAR & DELI

Lunch Nightly

636 Broadway
Kingston

Sultry bar. Twinkly courtyard. Unex-pected butcher case.

MODERN CLASSIC

Gaskin's

2 Church Ave
Germantown

Husband-wife Nick and Sarah Suarez focus on simple stun-ners made from local produce at their tiny town watering hole.

....

FARM DISTILLERY

Arrowood Farms

236 Lower Whitfield Rd
Accord

Bucolic brewery also crafts terroir-inspired vodka, gin, whiskey. Hosts indie club-worthy shows too.

....

BRUNCH

Bartlett House

2258 Hwy 66
Ghent

Railroad hotel circa 1870 now destination cafe. Parisian patio.

PAN-LATIN

Lil' Deb's Oasis

747 Columbia St
Hudson

Radically inclusive, queer-run Technicol-or tropicalia-tilting cafe-slash-all-day-party. Plus a wine menu to remember.

....

PIT STOP

Circle W

3328 Hwy 23A
Palenville

Postcard-perfect fill-up station with coffee, pancakes, sandwiches, gourmet groceries. Pre-hike fuel stop.

....

ICE CREAM

Del's Roadside

6780 Albany Post Rd
Rhinebeck

Vanilla-chocolate curlicue twists on a wafer cone.

CHEESE

Talbott & Arding
202 Allen St
Hudson

More like cheese concierge than counter. Deli-style dishes too.

....

BRAZILIAN-UKRAINIAN

MISTO
@n_misto_w

Wilson and Nadia Costa's pop-up draws on their respective heritages and home-grown ingredients.

....

TAPAS

Early Terrible
45 Mill Hill Rd
Woodstock

Woodsy willow-shaded garden for snacks and drinks.

....

BREWERY

Suarez Family Brewery
2278 US 9
Hudson

Concentration on complex lagers and "crispy" pales.

....

JAMAICAN

Top Taste
446 Hasbrouck Rd
Kingston

Look for lemon-lime shingles. Goat curry.

WINE LIST

Brunette
33 Broadway
Kingston

Romantic little nook for natural varieties.

....

PIZZA

Ollie's
4 Bruceville Rd
High Falls

Picnic tables with a view. Wood-fired and grandma-style pies.

....

DIVE BAR

Half Moon
48 S Front St
Hudson

DIY relic of a simpler [and cheaper] time in a rapidly changing city.

....

COFFEE & DOUGHNUTS

Historic Village Diner
7550 N Broadway
Red Hook

Hot and black in a mug. Dunk a powdered sugar-coated cake donut in.

....

JAPANESE

Quinn's
330 Main St
Beacon

Regular live music, bento boxes, katsu and stained-glass-lamp-lit booths.

CIDER

Left Bank Ciders
150 Water St
Catskill

Taproom to taste the nectar of both wild apples and those from small local orchards.

....

BEER & BOOKS

Spotty Dog
440 Warren St
Hudson

Grab a page-turner and a pint.

....

INDIAN

Cinnamon
1 E Market St
Rhinebeck

Sources veggies and meat from nearby farms for chaat, dosas and kebabs.

....

ROTISSERIE

Kitty's Market
60 S Front St
Hudson

Roast chicken plates plus a petite market. Flower-flocked yard.

....

OLD SCHOOL

Kozel's Restaurant
1006 Hwy 9H
Ghent

Czech family's third generation continues to fire the grill.

LODGING

MOUNTAIN RETREAT
Deer Mountain Inn
Tannersville
deermountaininn.com
Six-suite Arts &
Crafts cottage with
unceasing charm.
Toasty bar replete
with fireplace.
....

MAJESTIC VIEWS
Mohonk Mountain
House
New Paltz
mohonk.com
A fairytale-looking
castle. Possibly inspired
King's *The Shining*.
....

CATSKILLS CHALET
Scribner's Lodge
Hunter
scribnerslodge.com
Vegetable garden.
Barrel-shaped sauna.
Cozy library lounge.
....

SMALL-TOWN SUITE
Hotel Tivoli
Tivoli
hoteltivoli.org
Appointed in owners'
furniture collection.
Gallery-style shop.

IN-TOWN POSH
Hotel Kinsley
Kingston
hotelkinsley.com
Four separate 19th-
century buildings with
midcentury modern
furnishings scattered
across Kingston.
....

LOCALS IN THE LOBBY
Rivertown Lodge
Hudson
rivertownlodge.com
Once a downtown
movie house. Wood
fires in the common
space. Buzzy brunch.
....

RURAL RESORT
Callicoon Hills
Callicoon Center
callicoonhills.com
Revived Borscht Belt
beauty in fly-fishing
country. Massive pool.
....

HAMLET HIDEAWAY
The Graham & Co.
Phoenicia
thegrahamandco.com
Screen-free activity
list. Bikes, badminton,
swimming, s'mores.

ARTISTS WELCOME
Spruceton Inn
West Kill
sprucetoninn.com
Little white bunk-
house in the meadow.
Meet the season's
artists-in-residence by
the creekside firepit.
....

MOD MOTOR COURT
Starlite Motel
Kerhonkson
thestarlitemotel.com
Painted Day-Glo
pink and teal. Great
basecamp for hiking
and ski trails nearby.
....

RIVERFRONT MANOR
The Suminski Innski
Tivoli
suminskiinnski.com
Watch the sun rise and
set over the river on the
wraparound veranda.
....

COUNTRY ESTATE
Troutbeck
Amenia
troutbeck.com
Belonged to poet-
naturalist Breton
family. Picnic menu.

LODGING

Stewart House

Athens

stewarthouse.com

Elegant design around every corner. Fish frys, live music, tap takeovers keep the feel friendly not fussy.

....

IN HARMONY

Woodstock Way

Woodstock

woodstockway.com

Rustic-mod quarters straddle Tannery Brook off town's main drag.

....

LODGE LUXE

Urban Cowboy

Big Indian

urbancowboy.com

Easier to deal with no cell service in a copper bathtub overlooking Catskills.

....

BED & PIZZA

The Woodhouse Lodge

Greenville

thewoodhouselodge.com

Wood-fired pizza sleepover in the forest.

MODERN PASTORAL

Inness House

Accord

inness.co

Farmhouse inn plus 28 slate-black cabins tucked into the woods. Tennis, swimming, nine-hole golf course.

....

CULINARY DRAW

The DeBruce

Livingston Manor

thedebruce.com

Many menu ingredients grown or foraged for on property.

....

RETRO RESPITE

Sylvan Motor Lodge

Hillsdale

sylvanmotorlodge.com

Whole-property rental with 10 rooms and fully equipped kitchen, so bring the fam.

....

HOME IN THE WOODS

Cranberry Pond House

Livingston Manor

cranberrypondhouse.com

Painterly scenery. Potbelly stove. Peace rolling like a river.

RAILROAD REDUX

Modern Accord Depot

Accord

modernaccorddepot.com

A 1902 train station turned cheery 2/2 rental and artist gallery. Ticket window still intact.

....

ON THE WATER

The Roundhouse

Beacon

roundhousebeacon.com

Former textile mill sits atop Fishkill Creek's rushing rapids.

....

CONTEMPORARY CABIN

Hutton Brickyards

Kingston

huttonbrickyards.com

Glass-front cabins contrast with surviving kiln sheds from property's past.

....

HANDMADE INN

Red Rose Motel

Roscoe

theredrosemotel.com

Flea-market flare except where it counts [i.e., sheets]. Tiny tavern.

SHOPPING

ALL-IN-ONE

WYLDE Hudson
35 S 3rd St
Hudson
Cafe and shop with cottagecore dresses, denim, leather bags. Open-air Summer Saturdays Market a draw for local makers.

....

GOURMET MARKET

Otto's Market
215 Main St
Germantown
Stock up for the weekend and grab a sandwich from the deli.

....

RECORDS

Ever Records
68 Tinker St
Woodstock
New addition to musical town. Small but strong selection.

....

FINE-ART FRAMING

Walnut Hill
551 Warren St
Hudson
Regionally milled wood. Splined corner joinery. Exhibition quality.

FARM STAND

Montgomery Place Orchards
4283 Hwy 9G
Red Hook
Bard College now owns legacied farm. Seasonal waves bring apples, berries, flowers, veggies, herbs, more.

....

BOTTLE SHOP

Kingston Wine Co.
65 Broadway
Kingston
Fun-not-preachy focus on traditionally made. Budget friendly too.

....

BOUTIQUE

Mary MacGill
212 Main St
Germantown
Stocks pretty but practical pieces. Also designs ethereal jewelry.

....

HARDWARE

Hales Hardware & Home Supplies
199 Broadway
Newburgh
Home remodels, art projects, they got it.

UNUSUAL PRINT

Rodgers Book Barn
467 Rodman Rd
Hillsdale
A fantasy in the forest. Weathered two-story wood barn brimming with books. Cast-iron wood stove-warmed reading nooks.

....

FLY SHOP

Dette Flies
13 Main St
Livingston Manor
Family owned since 1928, in the birthplace of American fly fishing.

....

HOME GOODS

Sundry.
6036 Main St
Tannersville
Carries mountain-made ceramics, candles, clothing, etc.

....

BOOKSTORES

Magpie Bookshop
Catskill
Oblong Books
Millerton
Blenheim Hill Books
Hobart

ART & CRAFT

FESTIVAL
O+ Festival
Kingston
opositivefestival.org
Nonprofit funds medical insurance for artists, musicians who create weekend's worth of performances.

....

TEXTILES
Alison Charli Smith
Peekskill
saltandstill.com
Naturally dyed quilts in earthy shades, from indigo, walnut, madder root and osage.

....

FLORIST
Shuheng Ji
Germantown
athabold.com
Incorporates local foliage and blooms, like poppies and peonies.

....

SCULPTOR
Kris Perry
Hudson
krisperry.com
His large-scale, leggy kinetic creations dot the Valley.

HANDMADE PAINTS
R&F Paints
Kingston
rfpaints.com
Only U.S. manufacturer of encaustic paint, an ancient beeswax-and-resin-based recipe.

....

DANCE
Kaatsbaan
Tivoli
kaatsbaan.org
Incubator on 153-acre cultural park. Summer 2021 fest fused ballet and Patti Smith.

....

GALLERY
Mother Gallery
Beacon
mothergallery.art
Women-owned space. Contemporary art.

....

WOOL
New York State Sheep & Wool Festival
Rhinebeck
sheepandwool.com
Competitive yarn spinning. Shepherd talks. Ewe sale.

ANTIQUE RESTORATION
Quittner Antiques
Germantown
quittnerantiques.com
Ben Davidson and Pippa Biddle refinish, rewire and revive furniture in their barn studio.

....

ARTS CENTER
Basilica Hudson
Hudson
basilicahudson.org
Factory ruin now multidisciplinary venue for concerts, art exhibitions, etc.

....

GRAPHIC DESIGN
Woody Pirtle
Hudson
pirtledesign.com
Posterwork shown at MoMA and internationally.

....

FILM FESTIVAL
Hudson Valley Picture Show
upstatefilms.org
Traveling, months-long event. Crowd pleasers and indies.

OUTDOORS

KAYAK
Bannerman Castle
Beacon
bannermancastle.org
Launch from Little Stony Point and paddle past the island ruins of former arsenal.

....

FLY FISHING
Wulff School of Fly Fishing
Lew Beach
wulffschool.com
Started by the queen of fly fishing, Joan Wulff. Casting and trout-catching classes.

....

SOCCER GAME
Stockade FC
Kingston
stockadefc.com
Foursquare founder's semipro league plays at Dietz Stadium.

....

SKI SLOPE
Hunter Mountain
Hunter
huntermtn.com
Only slopes in world with 100 percent snowmaker coverage.

ROCK CLIMBING
EMS Climbing School
Gardiner
emsoutdoors.com
Scale the quartz bedrock of Shawangunk Ridge, a nationally envied climbing spot.

....

HIKING
Mohonk Preserve
Ulster County
mohonkpreserve.org
Start at newly opened Testimonial Gatehouse Trailhead.

....

WATERFALL
Kaaterskill Falls
Hunter
Suspended viewing platform to behold majesty of 260-ft. drop.

....

FARMERS MARKET
Kingston Farmers Market
Kingston
@kingstonfarmersmarket
Year-round source for Valley's freshest produce, fish, more.

PICTURE SHOW
Greenville Drive-In
Greenville
drivein32.com
A '50s remnant screening Oscar contenders, blockbusters in the shadow of Catskills.

....

WALKING TRAIL
Hudson River Skywalk
Catskill
hudsonriverskywalk.org
Stroll the vista between homes of Thomas Cole and Frederic Church.

....

GREEN SPACE
Poet's Walk Park
Red Hook
scenichudson.org
Popular for a reason. Trees and stone walls create natural "rooms."

....

FIRE TOWER
Catskill Center
Catskill Park
catskillcenter.org
Catskill Center volunteers maintain park's six lookouts.

EXPERTS

CONSERVATION

Rocci Aguirre
Scenic Hudson
Hudson Valley-born
policy and advocacy
director for Scenic
Hudson Land Trust
spanning 12 counties.
....

MUSIC CRITIC

Amanda Petrusich
@amandapetrusich
New Yorker staff writ-
er with Guggenheim
and Grammy nods.
Wrote book about
record collectors.
....

URBAN DISPLACEMENT

Kwame Holmes
@kwameholmes
Director of
Kingston Housing
Lab and Bard Col-
lege's human rights
scholar-in-residence.
....

PHOTOGRAPHY

Stephen Shore
stephenshore.net
An American icon in
color photography.
Captures subtle sparkle
in an ordinary scene.

MAPLE SYRUP

Ashley Ruprecht
Laurel & Ash Farm
Harvests maple sap
from five acres and
wood fires it to
conjure four distinct
flavor intensities.
....

ENERGY

Jessica O. Matthews
Uncharted Power
Poughkeepsie-raised
entrepreneur designs
infrastructure solu-
tions. Invented energy-
generating soccer ball.
....

PRESERVATION

Emily Majer
*White Clay Kill
Preservation*
None better in win-
dow restoration. Also
Tivoli's deputy mayor,
town historian.
....

PROGRESSIVE FARMING

Jalal Sabur
sweetfreedomfarm.org
Trains next genera-
tion of BIPOC farm-
ers and grows food for
the food insecure.

CIDER PRODUCTION

Megan Larmer
Glynwood
Leads nonprofit's
Cider Project. Provides
education, economic
resources for Valley
apple producers.
....

CULTURE COMMENTATOR

Luc Sante
lucsante.com
Strand Books clerk
became fixture of
magazine-writing
golden age. Now
author, professor.
....

MUSIC PRODUCER

Aaron Dessner
@aaron_dessner
Has collaborated
with Bon Iver, Tay-
lor Swift and Sharon
Van Etten in barn-
shaped studio.
....

BLACK HISTORY

Janus Adams
janusadams.com
Journalist and
chronicler of civil
rights. Hosts Radio
Catskill show.

CITIES & TOWNS

*The region is flocked with idyllic farming villages, reimagined small
towns and bustling cities . Here, ten communities to paint the picture.*

BEACON

A decade ago, a *New York Times* article observed the art-driven renewal underway here and presupposed the town's pie-eyed proponents were a bit too ambitious. Turns out, they weren't. Since DIA:BEACON, the massive contemporary art museum that revived a Nabisco box-printing factory, opened in 2003, it has become the concrete cri de coeur for a modern art city—a movement fostered by patterned-brick-and-gabled show space HOWLAND CULTURAL CENTER. Now, Beacon's Hopper-esque Main Street storefronts harbor a slew of shops, like Beacon Mercantile, and art galleries including MORPHICISM, Fridman Gallery and Beacon Artist Union. Ponder the work you've seen over a drink at the adjacent WONDERBAR BEACON [tufted banquettes, big garnish energy] and cocktail cannery Liquid Fables.

SWAP MEET	POPULATION: 13,968
Beacon Flea	COFFEE: Big Mouth Coffee Roasters
Vans and tents spill out caches of vintage and handmade.	BEST DAY OF THE YEAR: Second Saturday, year-round

HUDSON

Hudson saw the biggest net in-migration of any U.S. metro during 2020, as city dwellers escaped to its wide-open spaces and storybook-like downtown. But it was already changing in ways exciting and complicated [two groups to look into: Future Hudson and Hudson/Catskill Housing Coalition]. Balance a visit with new and old. Follow a rye scone or warming rice porridge at CAFE MUTTON with a walk down the HENRY HUDSON WATERFRONT PARK to see a still-active lighthouse from 1874. Break for lunch at The Cascades, a locally loved deli since '93, before a WARREN STREET stroll with a stop at beer bar-bookstore Spotty Dog, or meander for tropical libations at LIL' DEB'S OASIS. Listen for music as you pass by The Park Theatre, a 1920s theater slated for demo but saved by Hudson Valley son Shanan Magee.

SLEEPOVER STOP	POPULATION: 6,235
Batterby House	COFFEE: Supernatural Coffee + Bakery
Part culinary shop, part five-room bed-and-breakfast.	BEST DAY OF THE YEAR: Basilica SoundScape, September

KINGSTON

Reimagining itself since the British burned it [nearly] down in 1777, New York State's first capital plays palimpsest for its ever more diverse populace. Start out in the city's pre-Revolutionary Stockade District. Browse titles and grab coffee at ROUGH DRAFT BAR & BOOKS, in one of the oldest remaining stone buildings. Nearby Front Street is a gold coast of vintage clothing and furniture and KINGSTON BREAD + BAR weds cocktails and state-of-the-art baking in one cozy cafe. The waterfront Rondout District has a Sausalito vibe with a busy little marina [featuring the HUDSON RIVER MARITIME MUSEUM]. Find topflight bottles at Kingston Wine Co. and Hudson Valley makers at Clove & Creek, or walk out to Kingston Point Beach to join locals watching the boats pass as sunset lights up the eastern shore.

TROLLEY STOP	POPULATION: 23,070
The Trolley Museum	COFFEE: Village Coffee and Goods
Ride a mile and a half in a	BEST DAY OF THE YEAR:
vintage rail car to the river.	O+ Festival, October

NEW PALTZ

Equal parts hippie enclave, college town and adventure gateway, New Paltz wears its multiple personalities affably. See the New York Center for Jungian Studies across the street from a modern witchcraft shop. Set off down the twisty village streets, lined with historic homes, to courtyard-blessed HUCKLEBERRY restaurant and LAGUSTA'S LUSCIOUS COMMISSARY! [house-made chocolates and a zine library]. There's a healthy tie-dye-and-patchouli presence here by way of SUNY New Paltz, but it's tempered by INQUIRING MINDS and BARNER bookshops, streetwear at Crust and Magic, and Rock and Snow, a top spot for climbers pursuing the famed bedrock cliffs of the SHAWANGUNK RIDGE to the west. For a deeper look at the city's history, Historic Huguenot Street reframes its 17th-century settlement by centering stories of displaced Esopus Munsee people and enslaved people.

TRAIL STOP	POPULATION: 14,036
	COFFEE: Mudd Puddle Coffee Roasters
River-to-Ridge Trail	BEST DAY OF THE YEAR:
Off-road 6-mile loop for	Woodstock-New Paltz Art &
walking, running and biking.	Crafts Fair, May and September

RHINEBECK & RHINECLIFF

A college-ish town with the maturity of a tenured professor, Rhinebeck benefits from proximity to Bard College, without the typical town-gown trappings. Well, there is an indie movie house, UPSTATE FILMS, but it has a storied legacy starting in 1972 and brings lauded filmmakers to town. The restaurant scene is grown-up, too, from brasserie-oyster bar LE PETIT BISTRO to River & Post, the new provincial incarnation of cheeky gastropub Liberty Public House. The stalwart bars here go way back, like all the way to 1766 in the case of BEEKMAN ARMS tavern, and 1890 for the neon-lit Foster's Coach House. On the drive where Market Street [oh yeah, there's SAMUEL'S SWEET SHOP, the candy store Paul Rudd co-owns. Wild right?] turns to Rhinecliff Road, look for Rondout Lighthouse, built in 1915 and still shining.

MARKET STOP	POPULATION: 8,242
Rhinebeck Farmers' Market	COFFEE: The Epicurean
Sunday morning a rainbow of produce and more.	BEST DAY OF THE YEAR: Fall foliage starts to turn, September

CATSKILL

To explain the different energies on either side of the river, Valley dwellers point to Catskill, which sits opposite Hudson. Yes, compared to the train-serviced, Arcadian east side, Catskill appears a bit dark and mysterious under the shadow of the mountains. But the town has been anything but shuttered lately. In fact, newer additions, like MAGPIE BOOKSHOP, a dreamy periwinkle store selling used and nearly new tomes, feel like longtime staples. More businesses open seemingly every day, like brewery SUBVERSIVE, across Catskill Creek inside a former mechanic's garage—one of few that goes the extra mile to make their own malt. Follow the creek down to RAMSHORN-LIVINGSTON SANCTUARY, an old-as-time tidal marsh teeming with birds that soar alongside another fresh addition, the HUDSON RIVER SKYWALK. Just think if Thomas Cole could have stood there as he painted.

SHOP STOP	POPULATION: 3,814
Corduroy Shop	COFFEE: HiLo
Fabric shop specializes in vintage and one-of-a-kind bolts.	BEST DAY OF THE YEAR: Parade of Lights, November

WOODSTOCK

Famously not the site of the eponymous festival, Woodstock did have a version of that counterculture revelry, albeit in the early 1900s, thanks to Hervey White, who splintered from Byrdcliffe Arts Colony [the oldest continuously functioning art colony] to create a "scruffier" outfit: The Maverick Art Colony. Its mason bee house-like barn still stands as an active venue by the name MAVERICK CONCERTS [John Cage's "4'33"" happened here]. That visionary, ruffian spirit runs through the city like Tannery Brook under Tinker Street, which easily leads to similarly minded spots, like bookshop THE GOLDEN NOTEBOOK [say hi to Neville] and museums WAAM and The Center for Photography. For music, there's Bearsville Theater, part of Albert Grossman's creative compound, and Colony, which brings in nationally touring artists to its three-story ballroom, built in 1929.

DINNER STOP	POPULATION: 5,793
Silvia	COFFEE: Bread Alone Bakery
Out of a Nancy Meyers movie set,	BEST DAY OF THE YEAR:
wood-fired everything.	Woodstock Film Festival

TIVOLI

Tiny Tivoli was conceived in grand ambition. Named by Robert R. Livingston after Italy's bucolic escape for Roman rulers, the town's original blueprint wasn't built, but it does mirror its namesake in pastoral views. Despite a petite population, Tivoli has outsized international presence in art, especially ballet. KAATSBAAN CULTURAL PARK, a 153-acre riverside retreat, hosts the discipline's best year-round, seen during their Spring Festival [think Yo La Tengo meets Yannick Lebrun], now encompassing music and food. Downtown's graceful main street, lined by preserved structures and gardened homes, awaits with dinner at Hotel Tivoli's THE CORNER and a nightcap from Traghaven Whiskey Pub's Irish collection, the country's biggest.

BAKERY STOP	POPULATION: 1,012
Tivoli Bread and Baking	COFFEE: All That Java
Mark the season with a sour-cherry,	BEST DAY OF THE YEAR:
blackcap raspberry or apple pastry.	Apple trees bloom, May

MILLERTON

Crossroads towns are de facto magnets. No wonder Millerton sprang up where three rail lines once met amid richly rolling farmland. And no wonder now, 170 years later, the preserved 19th-century townscape calls again—this time, though, with a slow-simmer scene anchored by OBLONG BOOKS and the independent Moviehouse theater. There's a percolating shopping ecosystem too: for flaneurs, there are antique and vintage spoils at HUNTER BEE and Redux Millerton; Erika Rector's serenely rustic ceramics at her BES Studios; home goods at DEMITASSE and Charlotte Taylor; and top tins at flagship HARNEY & SONS FINE TEAS. While the train whistles have faded into history's mists, one line has metamorphosed into the 26-mile HARLEM VALLEY RAIL TRAIL. The restored 1911 Millerton train station now happens to house a real estate office, for crossroads dreamers.

SHOP STOP	POPULATION: 924
Westerlind	COFFEE: Irving Farm New York
Outdoor-loving, Nordic-forward fashion upstairs, bistro downstairs.	BEST DAY OF THE YEAR: Millerton Earth Day, April

COLD SPRING

Picture the perfect Upstate snow globe: a streetscape of 19th-century gems perched on the river's deepest cut and surrounded by the Hudson Highlands. That's Cold Spring in there. Built from riches of a Civil War-era foundry and thereafter genteelly occupied by artists, writers and their patronage, Cold Spring's present density of independent and artistically minded businesses may be the best in the region: yes, antique browsing up and down Main Street, but also Stephanie Doucette's playfully printed designs at SWING and Melanie Leonard's modern millinery at WYNONO & COMPANY, paper wonders at Supplies for Creative Living, artful botanica at WYLD, the insightful selection in cheerful environs at SPLIT ROCK BOOKS, and unfailingly practical inventory for the particular at Cold Spring General Store.

DIVE STOP	POPULATION: 1,775
Doug's Pretty Good Pub	COFFEE: Paulette Cold Spring
English-muffin burgers at a saloony bar. Claims "bongos, used cars, live bait."	BEST DAY OF THE YEAR: Putnam County Wine & Food Fest, August

ROAD TRIP

For an odyssey of Upstate landscapes, art, culture, music and history, start down in the lower valley and wander up to the mountains.

DAY 1

CONTEMPORARY ART CRAWL

The Hudson Valley's soaring scenery has inspired centuries of art, but a relatively recent cadre of museums lifts its reputation to new heights.

Nearly two centuries after Thomas Cole painted the Hudson River onto the map, a world-class collection of contemporary museums and sites inks a brilliantly bold line to trace on both sides of the water. Begin where modernist vision meets the landscape itself at STORM KING ART CENTER in New Windsor. Here, 500 rolling acres flanked by mountainsides are ongoingly reshaped for outsize works by David Smith, Richard Serra, Mark di Suvero, Maya Lin and, most recently, Sarah Sze, among others [rent bikes at the entrance to make passage among the giants a breezy pleasure]. Swing south to Bear Mountain Bridge and up picturesque Highway 9D to MANITOGA, the former estate of the American industrial designer Russel Wright, in Garrison. Book a tour of DRAGON ROCK, Wright's circa-1961 light-filled house, studio and surrounding quarry landscape, designed with architect David Leavitt, where both men's admiration of Japanese architecture and landscape design create sublime integration with the natural world. If you miss booking a tour, 4 miles of footpaths [designed by Wright] are open every day to the public and offer leafy glimpses into the site's singular essence. Pop back in time for coffee and a bite to eat along the charming 19th-century streetscape of artist-encampment Cold Spring, just 20 minutes north, which is also home to MAGAZZINO ITALIAN ART, an elegantly fashioned new arrival. Opened in 2017 by private collectors and spouses Nancy Olnick and Giorgio Spanu, Magazzino is a 20,000-square-foot showcase for their collection, from Italy's post-1960s arte povera movement through present day. Spanish architect Miguel Quismondo's design—a repurposing of a computer-manufacturing warehouse—honors industrial provenance while making bold space for a new century. And no better finish to miles of museum-going than DIA:BEACON, the jewel in the Dia Art Foundation's crown of 11 sites. Dia:Beacon introduced the world to reusing massive industrial spaces as museums—in this case, reinvigorating a moribund box-printing facility for cookies-and-crackers behemoth Nabisco. Opened in 2003, the museum also pioneered the idea of creating a gallery around a work—not the other way around—finely tuning spaces to works by Andy Warhol and Louise Bourgeois, Charlotte Posenenske and On Kawara, among others. Exit through the bookshop that's sumptuous with monographs and catalogs, but also poetry, artists' books and titles on contemporary culture and critical theory.

UP AND OUT INTO THE MOUNTAINS

Take hold of all that natural splendor with
both hands on a fishing rod, or fix both feet atop
a cliffside trail.

FLY FISHING

Lying low out in Sullivan County in the western Catskills is the birthplace
of American fly fishing, LIVINGSTON MANOR. Start out at The Catskill Fly
Fishing Center & Museum, featuring a bamboo rod-making shop and a
tribute to globally known local fly-fishing legend Joan Wulff. Book lessons
and guided trips at DETTE FLIES, the world's oldest family-run fly shop. If
you feel worn out afterward, Sunshine Colony has homey nooks for a glass
of wine and snacks.

HIKING

Amid the sheer, spectacular Shawangunk Mountains, MOHONK PRESERVE
has 75 miles of carriage roads and trails. Classic routes include the
Undercliff-Overcliff Loop [where you can watch rock climbers on belay],
BONTICOU CRAG and TABLE ROCKS. Note that hikers pay a day-use fee.

DAY 3

THE MUSIC RAMBLE

Note the fields, houses and barns that played a part in making American music history.

In a special report by *Rolling Stone*, the editors observed on the last day of Woodstock that "less than 30,000 were in attendance for this last gasp and most of them straggled off ... [past] the clutter of a civilization that had spanned its own eternity." A sonic cultural boom, the 1969 music festival still resonates far beyond the four days it took place, much the way the site's emerald fields stretch on forever into the horizon today. The once dairy farm, about 45 miles from the town of Woodstock, where 400,000 people created an Edenistic autonomous zone, is now the BETHEL WOODS CENTER FOR THE ARTS. Whirl through the flower-powered museum, where the story of how the festival came to fruition is just as fascinating as the actual event. Then walk down the sloping lawn to where the stage stood and add a rock to the stacks that dot its outline. Take sylvan Highway 209 past Arrowood Farm Brewery in Accord, site of the WOODSIST FESTIVAL, a chill annual gathering of campers with a lineup of artists like Kevin Morby and Laraaji [curated by band Woods and their leader, Stone Ridge resident Jeremy Earl], to the backroads of West Saugerties. Drive slow down dirt road Parnassus Lane through the thick woods [heed the signage and don't disturb the neighbors] toward Big Pink, the modest peach-colored house where The Band lived and conjured impossibly iconic songs like "The Weight." Prior to *Music From Big Pink*, it's where they created *The Basement Tapes* as Bob Dylan's backing band. BIG PINK is now available from its current owners and preservationists as a short-term vacation rental for fans to fully commune with the property's spirit, but note the aforementioned basement level is unfortunately off-limits. Just 5 miles southwest, LEVON HELM STUDIOS, started by The Band's Turkey Scratch, Arkansas-born drummer and singer, still hosts Helm's sanctified Midnight Rambles, even after his 2012 passing. Watching one of these intimate shows in the barn loft is worth a plane ticket, let alone a day's drive. Pull the Dylan thread a bit more at the BEARSVILLE CENTER, east of downtown Woodstock, a venue-anchored compound owned by his [and Joplin's, Odetta's and Peter, Paul & Mary's] manager Albert Grossman. Allen Ginsberg, Todd Rundgren and Gordon Lightfoot also walked these grounds. RADIO WOODSTOCK recently moved from Rundgren's Utopia Sound Stage there to a former Methodist church in nearby West Hurley. Unplug the aux cord and scan the airwaves for 100.1 FM. Let the songs of this place and the music they influenced be the soundtrack for the drive.

DAY 4	**FARM-FORWARD**
	Cruise up Highway 9G on the river's eastern shore to a progressively minded slice of Arcadia.

Welcome to the Valley's Valhalla for u-picking and market shopping, amid forward-thinking restaurants and small farms in an area with deep agrarian roots. Circa-1798 ROSE HILL FARM in Red Hook brings holistic growing practices to pick-your-own cherries, blueberries, and apples. In Germantown, find pasture-raised goat, raw honey and bone broth at DARLIN' DOE, and book a dinner reservation at nearby GASKIN'S, a leader in the locally sourced menu. Hang out in the cocktail garden under the tall trees at women-owned COOPER'S DAUGHTER SPIRITS at Olde York Farm in Claverack, which makes black-walnut bourbon, lilac liqueur and ramp vodka from nearby-harvested and foraged ingredients. This area is also rich in farms focused on racial equity, social justice, queer and BIPOC ownership and regenerative practices. Look to: Rock Steady Farm, Sweet Freedom Farm, Hearty Roots Farm and Stone House Grain.

DAY
5

HOTEL HOPPING IN THE MOUNTAINS

An area with a leisure-seeking legacy, the Catskills' new generation of resorts, hotels and inns has brought around a second golden age.

In 1872, *The New York Times* reported that in the Catskills "there is a delicious sense of remoteness; a feeling of the completeness of nature's most bountiful gifts of expression. ... [Tourists] will find here no modern hotel luxuries; no bells to ring; no waiters to conciliate; no baths to take unless they might fancy a plunge into the rushing foaming mountain stream that is calling all day from the twilight gorge." Today, the Catskills have had a hospitality resurgence through properties that combine rustic appeal with those once-lacking modern luxuries. But there's no need to haul a suitcase from spot to spot to take advantage of every stayover stunner [unless that's your bag]. Each one is dinner-reservation or bar-stop worthy.

....

DEER MOUNTAIN INN *Tannersville* Brimming with turn-of-the-century yet evergreen character. Seems equally plausible that Meryl Streep or Mark Twain might be sitting in the crazy-cozy, fireplace-lit lounge upstairs. Bring a bottle of wine and a blanket up to the top of the mountain.

SPRUCETON INN *West Kill* Artist residency and inn that bills itself as a bed-and-bar. A Room One [whiskey, maple syrup and lemon] warms up a chilly Friday or Saturday evening. Ace merch from co-owner, illustrator Steven Weinberg.

SCRIBNER'S LODGE *Hunter* A once motor court, now luxe lodge with Scando-minimalist shades. The barrel-shaped sauna is the only big-views competition for the restaurant, Prospect, which makes good use of the on-site garden [illustrated maps to its plots available].

CALLICOON HILLS *Callicoon Center* A hip homage to the heyday of the area's midcentury resorts. Fishing and hiking opportunities at every turn, but you might be lured into the king-sized azure pool first.

HASBROUCK HOUSE *Stone Ridge* Dutch Colonial stone house from the 1700s with a wisteria-cloaked garden suite [just in case, it's room 15]. Bistro and bar Butterfield turns the area's bounty into art-level edible sculpture.

THE NORTH BRANCH INN *North Branch* Convivial community tables in the tavern and backyard. Adirondack chairs for leaned-back stargazing around the firepit.

MORE THAN 30 ENTRIES ▷

ALMANAC

A deep dive into the cultural heritage of
the Hudson Valley & Catskills through news clippings,
timelines, writings and other historical hearsay

WHALING INDUSTRY

When trade conflicts between the newly independent Americans and the British ended whaling from New England ports after the Revolutionary War, savvy Nantucket merchant brothers Seth and Thomas Jenkins endeavored toward new waters. Traveling 130 miles up the Hudson, they docked at tiny Claverack Landing, which was later renamed Hudson after its 1875 chartering. Other families, including shipfitters, sailmakers, ropemakers, followed, together laying out the city's grid and forming plans to make it a major whaling and shipping center. Although farther from the Atlantic, business and the population boomed, inviting competition from the Hudson Whaling Company and three outfits from neighboring Poughkeepsie: the Newburgh, Dutchess and Poughkeepsie whaling companies. The surge was short-lived, however, as blubber was replaced by other fuels, like kerosene. The last whaling ship sailed from Hudson to the Atlantic in 1844.

Between the 17th and 19th centuries, both whale oil and whalebone were essential items to make machinery lubricant, lantern fuel, corsets and umbrellas, among other staples. Some whaling ship sailors took the teeth from the carcass and carved intricate portraits and scenes into the ivory, an art known as scrimshaw.

THE FRIED CHICKEN WAR

A poultry skirmish occurred when Philadelphia lawyer George Harding couldn't get a plate of fried chicken for his no-red-meat dieting daughter at Charles Beach's Catskill Mountain House. Beach told Harding if he wanted chicken so much, he should build his own hotel. He did. Less than a mile away, on the summit of South Mountain, in 1881. It dwarfed Beach's hotel. The *Rondout Courier* reported on another side effect of the spite hotel, on August 16, 1881, under the headline "Chicken Famine in the Catskills." The article goes on to say, "Chickens have been very scarce all season. The reason is understood to be that Harding gathers all that are big enough to waddle for his mountain house. He built the hotel because he couldn't get chicken when he wanted it at Beach's and now every guest at the Harding House is obliged to eat chicken three times a day. This leaves none for anybody else." Both men died in 1902, the end of the ego-feud.

🍎

HEIRLOOM APPLES

CALVILLE BLANC D'HIVER

"White Winter Calville" in French. A spicy, tart, uniquely shaped baking apple that has roots all the way back to 1598.

....

CHENANGO STRAWBERRY

Early summer-ripener with a red-berry aroma. A bite through the translucent skin reveals a juicy, tender, sharp-tasting interior. A long harvesting period, enjoy from June to September.

....

JONAGOLD

Born in the New York State Agricultural Experiment Station laboratory in 1953, this variety is a cross between a Golden Delicious and bluish-crimson Jonathan. Sauté in a pat of butter and a dash of cinnamon.

ASHMEAD'S KERNEL

A small, lumpy, misshapen odd-ball pockets some pear and banana notes. Its unseen beauty is in its bright-tasting juice, often used for fermenting hard cider.

....

COX'S ORANGE PIPPIN

Once England's most desired dessert apple. Its tasting notes range from anise to orange juice, although its name comes from its tangerine-hued blush. A parent stock to many cultivar children.

....

ESOPUS SPITZENBURG

Oblong, red-and-yellow skinned. A late-season arrival with crisp flesh, delicate striping and spotting throughout. Cold storage boosts flavor.

COLLEGES

The Hudson Valley is home to a number of higher-learning institutions, public and private, liberal arts and vocational. Below, a sampling of schools.

BARD COLLEGE	Annandale-on-Hudson	1860
CULINARY INSTITUTE OF AMERICA	Hyde Park	1946
MARIST COLLEGE	Poughkeepsie	1905
MOUNT SAINT MARY COLLEGE	Newburgh	1959
SUNY NEW PALTZ	New Paltz	1828
UNITED STATES MILITARY ACADEMY	West Point	1802
VASSAR COLLEGE	Poughkeepsie	1861

FLIES OF NOTE

American fly fishing was born in the trout-filled creeks and rivers latticing the Catskill Mountain range. Below, six iconic flies from the area's deep-standing tradition.

QUILL GORDON *Designed by Theodore Gordon*

Called "The Father of American Dry Fly Fishing," Gordon married his study of British techniques with his knowledge of insects in the Catskills to create flies that not only corresponded to the area's species, but also proved more buoyant and quicker in the water. The Quill Gordon, built to skitter, endures as his flagship in the Catskills style he invented.

....

HENDRICKSON *Designed by Roy Steenrod*

Steenrod, Gordon's disciple-protégé, named this game-changing, evergreen fly after one of Gordon's best customers, Albert Everett Hendrickson. The three-tailed mayfly that the fly imitates also took on "the Hendrickson" as its common name.

....

DETTE CADDIS *Designed by Mary Dette*

"The First Family of Catskill Fly Tying," Walter and Winifred Dette taught themselves to tie in the late '20s, before their daughter Mary joined them. Originally Winnie sold flies out of a cigar case at her parents' hotel. Today, Mary's son, Joe Fox, owns the family store in Livingston Manor.

....

ROYAL WULFF *Designed by Lee Wulff*

Patterned by Wulff who, with his wife Joan, became a Catskills fly-fishing legend. His Royal Wulff has consistently lured in trout since he created it in 1930. It's a key example of his hairwings made with bucktail or calf tail.

....

BLACKNOSE DACE *Designed by Art Flick*

Flick's famous bucktail streamer, a wet-fly pattern rather than dry, was first mentioned in his 1947 handbook, *Art Flick's New Streamside Guide*, which went on to become a classic reference.

....

CATSKILL CANNONBALL *Designed by John Bonasera*

"Catskill John," as he's called, is a contemporary in Catskills fly tying and teaches classes on the craft. His gold beadhead nymph fly made with pheasant tail is fashioned to sink quickly in a stream.

CATSKILLS FLY FISHING IN SIX FLIES!

QUILL GORDON

HENDRICKSON

DETTE CADDIS

ROYAL WULFF

BLACKNOSE DACE

CATSKILL CANNONBALL

ESOPUS WARS

Tension with the Esopus Munsee tribe of Lenape Indians was immediate when the Dutch erected a village and stockade in present day Kingston, then called Wiltwyck. Trade commenced between the groups, albeit uneasily. The Esopus came to rely on many goods—guns, iron, copper, wool cloth and alcohol, a provision prohibited by the New Netherlands leadership to be given to the tribe. One evening, a Dutch mob—mistaking revelry for aggression—attacked a group of Esopus who had drunk brandy earlier with settler-farmers who had hired them to work. In retaliation, the Esopus laid siege to Wiltwyck, attacking livestock and destroying crops. War didn't end until July 1660, when the reinforced Dutch struck a truce with the Esopus. Three years of tentative peace ended, however, when the Esopus returned on June 7, 1663, and committed what would become known as the Esopus Massacre. Under the auspices of trade, the Lenape entered Wiltwyck and, in the words of Dutch Captain Martin Kregier, who wrote one of the few surviving records of the ordeal, "immediately fired a shot and made a general attack on our village from the rear, murdering our people in their houses with their axes and tomahawks and firing on them with guns and pistols; they seized whatever women and children they could catch and carried them prisoners outside the gates." With hostages, the Esopus retreated into the woods. The Lenape enlisted aid from the Minisink tribe, while the Dutch sent reinforcements upriver from New Amsterdam, as well as some Mohawk tribe members to help rescue the captives, and throughout the summer, a brutal game of cat and mouse played out. In September, the Dutch found the new Esopus holdout, killing their tribal leader, Papequanaehen. Resources exhausted, the Dutch ceded the territory to the British later that year. Though the Esopus signed treaties with the British establishing codes for trade and passage, as a result of the wars and more European settlement, they ceased to exist as a unified tribe. The few who remained crossed the Shawangunks to live among the Mohawk and other tribes. Some of their descendants are now part of the Stockbridge-Munsee Community in Wisconsin.

The 1655 Nicolls Treaty between the Esopus and British was infrequently renewed, but in one noted recommitment to peace more than 45 years later, tribal leaders presented a wampum belt to Ulster County justices with the message, "We are all brethren and what befalls one shall befall the other."

TREES OF NOTE

AMERICAN BEECH *Fagus grandifolia* Shady, offering sustenance for woodland creatures with its beechnuts. Ranges from 50-120 ft. tall.

SUGAR MAPLE *Acer saccharum* Dazzling foliage in autumn, distinctive grain patterns, sap for all syrup needs.

YELLOW BIRCH *Betel alleghaniensis* Massive candelabra form, curly, translucent bark. Golden blaze of leaves in autumn.

RED MAPLE *Acer rubrum* Dense, fibrous root network prevents other plants from growing near its trunk. Early settlers made ink and dye from bark extract.

BLACK CHERRY *Prunus serotina* Crushed leaves have a cherry-like odor and bitter taste reveals toxic amygdalin. Bark used for cough medicine, wood for furniture, and fruit for jelly and wine.

AMERICAN BASSWOOD *Tilia americana* Favored by bees, with the moniker "bee-tree"; produces a strongly favored honey. Indigenous people used tough inner bark for ropes, woven mats.

WHITE PINE *Pinus strobus* Cuts a solemn, straight figure of anywhere from 70-100 ft. Once the most valuable tree in Northeast for construction, and trunks were prized for ship masts in the colonial period.

HEMLOCK *Tsuga canadensis* Pendulous limbs and short-needled, feathery branches. Bark contains tannins formerly used in leather production.

EASTERN HOP-HORNBEAM *Ostrya virginiana* Robust constitution, the hard and tough native wood once used for sleigh runners.

MOUNTAIN MAPLE *Acer spicatum* Small, durable. Vital in preventing erosion of streambanks and steep slopes. Indigenous tribes boiled twigs with alum to soothe smoke-irritated eyes.

PIN CHERRY *Prunus pensylvanica* Seedlings that come up after a forest-fire lend the nickname "fire cherry." A "nurse" tree, it provides cover and shade for seedlings of next generation, larger hardwoods.

> *In 2019 researchers from SUNY Binghamton identified the world's oldest known living forest, in Cairo, NY. The Paleozoic forest showcased three different fossilized tree species, including the Archaeopteris, a genus researchers believe produced the first modern tree.*

THE BORSCHT BELT

Oppressive summer heat in the cities, widespread antisemitism, grim working conditions and hotel policies barring Jewish guests in the first half of the 20th century made the cool climes of the Catskills an amiable trade for Jewish vacationers. Decades of resort- and inn-building gave rise to "The Borscht Belt," a colloquial term used to describe the collection of Jewish lodging scattered across the mountains [other nicknames: "Jewish Alps" and "Sour Cream Sierras"]. Named after the classic Russian beet soup regularly found on resort menus, the area had nearly 600 hotels, 500 bungalow colonies and 1,000 rooming houses. From Sullivan to Ulster County, spots like the Concord, the Pines and the Laurels had storied luxury and swagger. The Concord alone had 40 tennis courts, three golf courses, 1,200 guest rooms, a dining room for 3,000 and its own gas station. Nearby Grossinger's [described in Modercai Richler's 1965 *Holiday* travel essay as "Disneyland with knishes"] had its own post office and air strip. Another activity not exactly on the official list at these resorts: matchmaking. Concord maître d' Irving Cohen, "King Cupid of the Catskills," was reported to have an uncanny sensibility for who to seat next to whom at dinner. But The Belt was perhaps most famous for its stages that gave talent like Lenny Bruce, Mel Brooks, Joan Rivers and Rodney Dangerfield their first gigs. By 1959, rising Jewish assimilation, the advent of air-conditioning, cheap airfare and television all contributed to the slow shutter of many properties, even those with generations-deep legacy guests. The Concord was ultimately bulldozed in 1998. But The Borscht Belt was always more than a place; in its heyday, it was an engine of American Jewish culture.

Three season-two episodes of the Emmy-winning comedy series The Marvelous Mrs. Maisel *follow burgeoning stand-up comedian Midge Maisel [played by Rachel Brosnahan] and her family as they escape the New York City summer for the fictional Steiner Mountain Resort, with Midge booking gigs at venues like the Concord. The episodes meticulously depict a sprawling camp filled with endless activities, beauty parlor gossip, nightly shows and plenty of family drama.*

FIRE TOWERS

A combination of drought, lightning, logging, quarrying and steam-engine ashes ignited many a fire in the early 1900s. To spot the flames early, New York built over 100 fire towers throughout the state between 1908 and 1950, with 23 of them in the Catskills. Today, five remain in Catskill Park—all on the National Register of Historic Places. Below, a list of towers, from oldest to newest. All are accessible via hiking trails and still offer the best views of the mountains. The Arkville-based Catskill Center and a team of volunteers maintain them and host regular tours.

BALSAM LAKE MOUNTAIN .... 3,723 ft.
Wood version raised in 1887. Present steel tower, 1930. *Hardenburgh*

HUNTER MOUNTAIN .... 4,040 ft.
Log tower built in 1909. Steel version put up 1917. *Hunter*

TREMPER MOUNTAIN .... 2,740 ft.
Original tower from 1917. *Shandaken*

RED HILL .... 2,990 ft.
Current structure built 1921. *Denning*

OVERLOOK MOUNTAIN .... 3,140 ft.
Built in 1927 on Gallis Hill. Moved in 1950. *Woodstock*

PINKSTER

Like New York State itself, Pinkster was born Dutch but transformed into something else. At spring's Pentecost, dancing and merriment would break out in the colony alongside more sober, churchy doings. By the 1700s, the festival became a crack in slavery's facade, embraced by the area's enslaved African people as a chance to travel, celebrate and commune. Black Pinkster evolved its own rituals—the drums of the Guinea dance, the building of temporary structures bearing traces of African design— and acclaimed its own monarch. In Albany, site of the greatest Pinkster, the ruler was known as King Charles. In 1803, a "Pinkster Ode" addressed the king: "At Pinkster, flow'rs will deck the field / And pleasures sweet will banish pain / Love-broken-hearts shall all be heal'd, / Although they may be crack'd again." Just a few years later, in 1811, Albany city government banned Pinkster, perhaps unnerved by the large gathering of enslaved people. Of late, revival efforts have awakened the Pinkster revels.

EDITH WHARTON

Although she became the first woman to win the Pulitzer Prize, in 1921 for her *Age of Innocence*, Edith Wharton was forbidden to read novels until after she was married. Born Edith Newbold Jones, much of her childhood played out at Wyndcliffe, her family's palatial Norman-style summer home in Rhinecliff, which in American legend inspired the phrase "keeping up with Joneses." Wharton harbored no sentimentality for the home [which has long sat abandoned and crumbling on the banks of the Hudson River], nor many people from that time either. "I never exchanged a word with a really intelligent human being until I was over twenty," she wrote. As for the house, she said: "The effect of terror produced by the house at Rhinecliff was no doubt due to what seemed to me its intolerable ugliness. I can still remember hating everything at Rhinecliff, which, as I saw, on rediscovering it some years later, was an expensive but dour specimen of Hudson River Gothic." Wyndcliffe sold for $120,000 in 2016, and sold yet again the next year to another buyer, but it remains in ruins and a candidate for demolition.

THE CLERMONT

Old Steamboat Days on the Hudson River
By David Lear Buckman, 1907

Robert Fulton will always be known as the inventor of the steamboat. It was a great day in the world's work, when, after years of study, experiment and disappointment, he traveled from New York to Albany on his little steamboat the *Clermont*. That was in August, 1807, just one hundred years ago. A new distinction was added to the noble Hudson, that of being the first river on which a successful demonstration of steam navigation had been made. There had been previous efforts made both in this country and abroad to apply the steam engine, yet in the infancy of its development, to the navigation of boats, but without practical results. Fulton himself made a trial on the Seine, France, in 1803, and failed. The boat was too frail to stand the weight of the engine and boilers and they had broken through the bottom of the craft during an overnight storm and sunk in the river. Others had tried before him. ... It remained for Fulton to inaugurate on the Hudson the system of navigation that was to revolutionize the carrying trade of the world.

DIRTY DANCING

The 1987 rom com, with stars Jennifer Gray and Patrick Swayze steaming up the Catskills, created an unexpected legacy of touring musicals, pop-culture tributes and social analysis. Critical takes from three eras:

The title and the ads seem to promise a guided tour into the anarchic practices of untrammeled teenage lust, but the movie turns out to be a tired and relentlessly predictable story of love between kids from different backgrounds.

—ROGER EBERT 1987

The West End is alive—well, sometimes—with the sound of musicals: Broadway transfers, homegrown revivals, and, in the case of "Dirty Dancing," a local premiere that isn't so much a fully conceived stage production as it is a tedious replicate-by-numbers version of a pre-existing film. Is that something to sneer at? Not in the eyes of ticketholders, apparently, who before the show's opening at the Aldwych Theatre two weeks ago had already coughed up more than $20 million for advance tickets.

—MATT WOLF *International Herald Tribune*, 2006

Look beyond the deceptively raunchy opening credits and you'll realise that the steamy romance was all just a clever vehicle for a critical, social and political portrait of American life in the '60s, and that *Dirty Dancing* is, in fact, an enduring piece of feminist cinema. ... In a cinematic climate filled with machismo, *Dirty Dancing* was one of the only films where a leading female character—an awkward, opinionated virgin no less— possessed the agency to change the lives of the people in her life.

—LARA C. CORY *Little White Lies*, 2017

The film's screenplay used Grossinger's Resort Hotel, one of the Catskills' grandest vacation spots, as the inspiration for the fictional Kellerman's. Today, most of the land the now-abandoned property sits atop is indeed dirty. In 2017, a new owner applied for 72 acres to be designated a brownfield to start remediating the contaminated soil. Lifted hopes to revive the resort remain up in the air.

WOODSTOCK

*The National Anthem often heralds the beginning of things to come,
but at Woodstock, it was the last sound that echoed over the field.*

Billed before its August 1969 unfolding as "an aquarian exposition in White Lake, NY. Three days of peace and music," Woodstock remains a watershed moment in counterculture history—near literally as festival goers persevered through lines of storms that turned the site into a mud pit. But Woodstock almost didn't happen. Planning the party before securing the venue, the four promoters failed a few times to find a site large enough to host the event when residents in the town of Woodstock and several other proposed sites balked at the idea of hosting so many hippies. Then, one promoter met Max Yasgur, owner of a 600-acre dairy farm outside Bethel, nearly 60 miles from the festival's namesake. His view: "Look, the reason you don't want them here is because you don't like what they look like. And I don't particularly like what they look like either. But that's not the point. They may be protesting the war, but thousands of American soldiers have died so they can do exactly what they're doing. That's what the essence of the country is all about." The sentiment reverberates eerily in the recording of Jimi Hendrix's now-iconic performance of "The Star-Spangled Banner"—the last of the festival, but perhaps the most memorable. With every quicksilver slide down his fretboard and tremor of his whammy bar, 26-year-old Hendrix, once a member of the 101st Airborne Division, conjured the violence of the Vietnam War inside the regimented melody—people screaming, helicopters overhead, bombs truly bursting in air. All of this played out at 8:30 in the morning. Hendrix had been scheduled to go on last the night before, but the chaos of pushing performers onto the stage bumped his time past sunrise. A report from *Rolling Stone* editors on the ground among the dwindling audience that remained: "And finally and finally, at 8:30, Jimi Hendrix in turquoise and white, in velvet and suede … brought it all crashing to a two-hour close. … It's like watching God perform the Creation. 'And for my next number …'"

Later that year on The Dick Cavett Show, *Cavett told Hendrix he expected hate mail after talking about his "unorthodox" anthem. Hendrix retorted, "It's not unorthodox! I thought it was beautiful." Cavett later conceded that "we should decorate Hendrix" for turning the "most dismal … dirge of a national anthem" into music. Hendrix died a year later at 27.*

THE PEEKSKILL RIOTS

In September 1949, *a huge racist mob attacked a concert by singer Paul Robeson, a Black icon associated with activist and communist politics. Police allegedly stood by or even aided the mob. Commentary from long-running Black newspaper* The New York Age:

"AIN'T NO CHAINS CAN BIND ME"—ROBESON

An aroused Paul Robeson was in the city this week busy mapping an ambitious program against the would-be lynchers who tried to break up his concert at Peekskill, N.Y., Sunday afternoon with a police-assisted riot. Elevated to the status of a martyr through the dumb, amazing stupidity of police and other law enforcement officials, the Robeson campaign is shaping itself as a gigantic protest vehicle against the flaming injustices, violence and rigid discrimination oppressing Negroes everywhere. Responsible citizens, of both races, shocked at the bunglesome manner in which the whole matter was held, are flooding Gov. Dewey at Albany with protests and demands for a sweeping investigation into the queer police tactics which, aside from allowing a full-fledged riot to rage for five hours, also made hundreds of thousands forget all about identifying Robeson with Communism and see him as a victim of Negro persecution. Action of the state troopers and police assigned to the concert grounds at old Hollow Brook Country Club in Peekskill has backfired. Robeson is as explosive now as a stick of dynamite.

MARY JOSEPHINE WALTERS

The biggest names among the Hudson River painters turn up anywhere and everywhere. Bierstadt, Moran, Church boldly romanticized the landscapes before them, from *The Great Chasm of Colorado* to *The Heart of the Andes*. Mary Josephine Walters, by comparison, stayed close to home, quietly seeking the glories of the Catskills, New Jersey, or New York's great river itself. Though she operated a city studio for years and created notable works, the first line of every biography on Walters emphasizes how little is known of her. Still, she leaves a legacy like the inner glow of her *Forest Interior*: soft but strong.

HENRY HUDSON

*In 1691, the English navigator Henry Hudson, sailing for
Dutch interests aboard the* Halve Maen, *explored the river that would
bear his name. A crewman's journal:*

The third Voyage of Master HENRIE HUDSON
Written by ROBERT JUET of Lime-house.

SEPT. 13. Faire weather, the wind Northerly. At seven of the clocke in the morning, as the floud came we weighed, and turned foure miles into the River. The tide being done wee anchored. Then there came foure Canoes aboord : but suffered none of them to come into our ship. They brought great store of very good Oysters aboord, which we bought for trifles.

SEPT. 14. Very faire weather, the wind South-east, we sayled up the River twelve leagues, and had five fathoms ; and came to a Streight betweene two Points. The River is a mile broad. The Land grew very high and Mountainous. The River is full of fish.

SEPT. 15. The morning was misty untill the Sunne arose : then it cleered. So wee weighed with the wind at South, and ran up into the River twentie leagues, passing by high Mountaines. Wee had a very good depth, and great store of Salmons in the River. At night we came to other Mountaines, which lie from the Rivers side. There wee found very loving people, and very old men : where wee were well used.

SEPT. 17. Faire Sun-shining weather, and very hot. In the morning as soone as the Sun was up, we set sayle, and ran up six leagues higher, and found shoalds in the middle of the channell, and small Ilands, but seven fathoms water on both sides.

> *The Hudson River, navigable from New York Harbor to present-day Troy,
> proved the central trading artery for the Dutch colony of New Netherland,
> and remains a vital cargo route. Hudson himself explored vast tracts of
> North America before being set adrift by his own mutinous crew.*

ELEANOR ROOSEVELT

Orphaned at 10 years old and raised by relatives in Tivoli, First Lady Eleanor Roosevelt remained tied to the Hudson Valley and resided partially at the Roosevelt family estate in Hyde Park, even after her husband became president. From 1935 to 1962, she wrote a national syndicated column, My Day, where she deftly wove relatable moments of her personal life with her unprecedented dealings as a woman in current events, political issues and global policy. The landscape she loved often figured into her text. Below, selections from her column.

"The Human Rights Commission, in part at least, had lunch with me at Hyde Park yesterday. For the second time this year we were blessed with a most beautiful day, and so had a very successful outdoor picnic. Though not quite as warm as the last time when I entertained the members of Committee Three, it was balmy enough for everybody to have a pleasant time sitting around the swimming pool in the sun. I find that people from other nations like our Hudson River landscape. When I take them up and show them the cottage where my son and his wife now live, but which my husband built, they are always enchanted by the view of the Catskill Mountains in the distance." *May 23, 1949*

···

"The other day I had a talk with a fruit stand owner who is active in local politics on the west side of the Hudson River. He told me that he wished more political bigwigs could get down and understand the local picture. ... This desire for identification with the people who are actually dealing with important events in our country is something quite understandable and I think something that all candidates should take into consideration." *July 16, 1956*

···

"There is something about a storm which I much enjoy. I would rather be out walking, for I like the physical feeling of battling the wind and the drive of rain in my face. There is a sense of struggle with nature which, I think, arouses in all of us an elementary desire to enter the battle. I spent my early childhood opposite the Catskill Mountains, where we were trained to look on thunderstorms as something rather beautiful to watch and were told the old legend of Henry Hudson and his men playing bowls. This early training has removed my fears, so I do not want to take refuge indoors and can admire the grandeur of the storm." *July 13, 1938*

WHITMAN AND BURROUGHS

Poet friends Walt Whitman and John Burroughs often met at Burroughs'
Hudson Valley home. Below, summertime verse by both.

"Happiness and Raspberries"
By Walt Whitman

June 21—HERE I am, on the west bank of the Hudson, 80 miles north of New York, near Esopus, at the handsome, roomy, honeysuckle-and-rose-embower'd cottage of John Burroughs. The place, the perfect June days and nights, [leaning toward crisp and cool,] the hospitality of J. and Mrs. B., the air, the fruit, [especially my favorite dish, currants and raspberries, mixed, sugar'd, fresh and ripe from the bushes—I pick 'em myself—the room I occupy at night, the perfect bed, the window giving an ample view of the Hudson and the opposite shores, so wonderful toward sunset, and the rolling music of the RR. trains, far over there—the peaceful rest—the early Venus-heralded dawn—the noiseless splash of sunrise, the light and warmth indescribably glorious, in which, [soon as the sun is well up,] I have a capital rubbing and rasping with the flesh-brush—with an extra scour on the back by Al. J., who is here with us—all inspiriting my invalid frame with new life, for the day. Then, after some whiffs of morning air, the delicious coffee of Mrs. B., with the cream, strawberries, and many substantials, for breakfast.

Excerpt from "June's Coming"
By John Burroughs

How soft the landscape near and far!
A shining veil the trees infold;
The day remembers moon and star;
A silver lining hath its gold.

Again I see the clover bloom,
And wade in grasses lush and sweet;
Again has vanished all my gloom
With daisies smiling at my feet.

Again from out the garden hives
The exodus of frenzied bees;
The humming cyclone onward drives,
Or finds repose amid the trees.

At dawn the river seems a shade—
A liquid shadow deep as space;
But when the sun the mist has laid,
A diamond shower smites its face.

SOJOURNER TRUTH

Abolitionist and activist Isabella Baumfree was born into slavery in Ulster County and spoke only Dutch until she was sold to another man in Kingston. She escaped a year before the state granted emancipation and took the name Sojourner Truth after she experienced a vision where God called her to preach. Shortly after, in 1828, she even won back custody of her son in court from his enslaver in Alabama. Truth delivered her most famous speech, "Ain't I a Woman?," in 1851 at the Ohio Women's Rights Convention. Completely extemporaneously she said, "That man over there says that women need to be helped into carriages, and lifted over ditches, and to have the best place everywhere. Nobody ever helps me into carriages, or over mud-puddles, or gives me any best place! And ain't I a woman? Look at me! Look at my arm! I have ploughed and planted, and gathered into barns, and no man could head me! And ain't I a woman? I could work as much and eat as much as a man—when I could get it—and bear the lash as well! And ain't I a woman? I have borne thirteen children, and seen most all sold off to slavery, and when I cried out with my mother's grief, none but Jesus heard me! And ain't I a woman? … If my cup won't hold but a pint, and yours holds a quart, wouldn't you be mean not to let me have my little half measure full?"

WASHINGTON IRVING

Born last of 11 and quite frail through his childhood, Washington Irving shirked school for adventure stories and drama. During a yellow fever outbreak, he traveled up the Hudson to Tarrytown. There he had his first encounter with Dutch culture and ghost stories told by Sleepy Hollow locals. He also traveled through the Catskill Mountains, the setting for "Rip Van Winkle." A passage below.

In a long ramble of the kind on a fine autumnal day, Rip had unconsciously scrambled to one of the highest parts of the Kaatskill mountains. He was after his favorite sport of squirrel shooting, and the still solitudes had echoed and re-echoed with the reports of his gun. … From an opening between the trees he could overlook all the lower country for many a mile of rich woodland. He saw at a distance the lordly Hudson, far, far below him, moving on its silent but majestic course, with the reflection of a purple cloud or the sail of a lagging bark, here and there, sleeping on its glassy bosom, and at last losing itself in the blue highlands.

INDIGENOUS PLACE NAMES

For thousands of years prior to European colonization, the Hudson Valley and Catskill Mountains were home to a host of Algonquin and Iroquois Native American tribes, among others, including the Lenni-Lenape, Mohican, Wappinger and the subset groups within them. Before Henry Hudson's arrival, the Lenape called the Hudson River Muhheakantuck, which means "the river that runs both ways"—just one example of the many Indigenous designations erased. Although many tribes were decimated by settlers and forced to move west from Upstate New York, there are still several towns and sites that carry their original names or transliterations of them today.

NAPANOCH .... *land overflowed by water*

COPAKE .... *snake pond*

COXSACKIE .... *hoot-owl place*

POUGHKEEPSIE .... *the reed-covered lodge by the little-water place*

ESOPUS .... *high banks*

SHANDAKEN .... *land of rapid waters*

SHAWANGUNK .... *in the smoky air*

TAGHKANIC .... *in the trees*

WAPPINGER .... *easterner*

WASSAIC .... *narrow valley*

MILTON GLASER

In his house at 148 Lewis Hollow in Woodstock, internationally influential graphic designer Milton Glaser created some of American culture's most recognizable imagery. In 1966, after Bob Dylan decamped to Woodstock following a motorcycle accident, Glaser was asked to create a poster for Dylan's upcoming *Greatest Hits* album. Atop a silhouette profile, Glaser twirled the songwriter's signature curls into Technicolor locks. But it was in 1977 that he created his landmark "I ♥ NY" logo for New York State's Division of Tourism. He sketched it on an envelope in a taxicab, but refined the work in his home studio at the same desk he dreamed up the Dylan poster. The tourism board also commissioned his Catskills poster with a gray tabby peeking out from the mountains. Glaser's kitchen table also has claim to fame by way of Townes Van Zandt's 1969 self-titled album cover.

PETE SEEGER

In the Hudson Valley, Pete Seeger is known as an activist not only in folk music but also conservation. Spurred by reading Silent Spring *in 1962 and the ongoing pollution of the Hudson River, he built* The Clearwater, *part boat, part environmental education vehicle.*

"When the ship was finished, there were strong arguments about how it should be run. … We voted to make the purpose of the Clearwater [as we called the sloop] helping to restore the [Hudson] river and its shores. The Clearwater is a highly visible symbol which says: Somebody is trying to do something about the river. Part of the problem is keeping our struggle visible. The Clearwater has done this by serving as an object of beauty like a temple. It is a supremely beautiful construction of wood, canvas, and rope. People look at it from the shore and say, 'That's the Clearwater! Those are the people trying to clean up the river!' Every spring and summer we take school children out, charging the local school board a flat price. The biologist ondeck shows the kids how much life is now present in the river by bringing from out of the water a fine mesh net and showing through a microscope what it contains. … The river has gradually been improving. We can't claim all the credit as we are just a part of a nationwide revulsion which took place in the late 1960s and early 1970s against pollution. The Federal Clean Water Amendment of 1972 was passed as a result of this movement. … We also raise money and hire lawyers and scientists and along with other organizations go to court to stop polluters. We've joined with the fishermen of the Hudson River and have gotten polluters to stop putting PCB into the river. … I'm tremendously impressed with the resiliency of the American people, but I'm not optimistic as we go into the next decade. Americans tend to underestimate the difficulties ahead of us, as probably does the whole human race. If people knew ahead of time how difficult it was to raise a family or put up a house, they would probably be too discouraged to start. Recently I went to a convention of biologists and met some healthy young people who have decided not to bring children into the world. They said they know what shape the environment is in and feel discouraged they haven't gotten the rest of the world to listen and change. But I told them that I've seen people's heads turn a hundred and eighty degrees within a few hours. Sometimes music has done it. Sometimes a great oration has done it. Sometimes reading a book has done it." —*Pete Seeger Box 431 Beacon, NY 12508*

LOOMIS SANITARIUM

Driven by a belief that tuberculosis could not survive high altitudes and fresh air could relieve those suffering from the widespread, then-incurable disease, many rode the rails, river and roads to the Catskills in the early 20th century to quarantine and heal at resort-style hospitals. One such sanitarium commemorated Dr. Alfred Loomis, who, combining his study of autoinoculation with his own personal experience, began the process of building a recovery resort—a vision brought to fruition by banking mogul J.P. Morgan, whose wife died of TB just three months after they wed.

THE BOSTON MEDICAL AND SURGICAL JOURNAL
Thursday, June 24, 1897

THE LOOMIS SANITARIUM FOR CONSUMPTIVES, AT LIBERTY

The first annual report of the Loomis Sanitarium for Consumptives [Liberty, Sullivan Co., N.Y. with hospital and dispensary at 230 West 38th Street, New York City] has just been published. The late Dr. Alfred L. Loomis, of whom the Sanitarium is a memorial, the report states, had pronounced views in regard to the arresting and cure of incipient phthisis by climatic treatment, and repeatedly sent patients to Colorado, the Adirondacks, and Liberty, with results proving the correctness of his views. The great distance to Colorado and the limited accommodations at Saranac made it difficult for some invalids to avail themselves of either place. Liberty then suggested itself to Dr. Loomis as an ideal situation for the erection of a sanitarium, where patients, after a four hours' journey from New York, could find themselves 2,200 feet above the sea-level, in air shown by scientific tests to be the equal of Colorado and the Adirondacks for the treatment of phthisis. The renting of a small house in West 38th Street, New York, for a city hospital and dispensary, was soon followed by the purchase of 193 acres of land two miles west of Liberty, where it was hoped in the near future to build a sanitarium. Then came the lamented death of Dr. Loomis, and, following it, the noble gift of the Sanitarium as a memorial of him by Mr. J. Pierpont Morgan. ... The object of the Sanitarium is to help persons in the incipient stages of phthisis recover their health who, by reason of limited means, are unable to go to more expensive resorts, or to travel long distances. ... The Sanitarium promises either a complete cure, or such an improved condition that they can return to their homes and be able to carry on their work.

INCLUDED

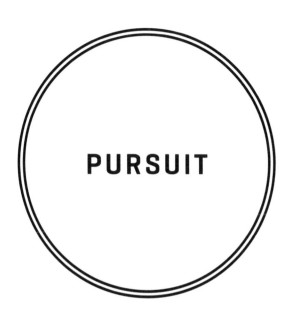

PURSUIT

A field guide to art and antiques in the Hudson Valley
& Catskills from museums to markets, with historical
background, cultural insight, auction advice and more

ART & ANTIQUES

"We are still in Eden," painter Thomas Cole wrote in 1836 of his Hudson Valley home. Since 8,000 B.C.E., the thick forests, rolling hills, soaring mountains and the Hudson River itself have provided resources, respite and revelations for diverse peoples—from Native tribes to Dutch settlers and Palatine German refugees to Jewish resort-builders. Centuries-old architecture and craftwork still endure here, as does an appreciation for them. But the region is most famous for the art it inspired Cole, and a cadre of other artists, to capture on canvas.

FOUNDATIONS

ART

Said to be the United States' first true artistic fraternity, the Hudson River School refers to the 19th-century artists who flocked to this piece of Arcadian land to paint its mythological beauty. Cole, Asher Brown Durand, Frederic Edwin Church and John Frederick Kensett represent some of its more renowned names. More recently, this same landscape has become the art as contemporary sculptors create pieces facilitated by its volume, as seen at museums like Art Omi and Storm King.

ANTIQUES

Antiques take time—100 years to be exact, according to scholars—and the region's long history of grand homes and humble farmsteads has led to an astounding inventory. Shops and auction houses have attracted experts, with interests that reach far beyond the region, who have brought their collections with them. Today, there are few better places to immerse yourself in the artifacts of lives once lived.

ARCHITECTURE

The architecture in the Hudson Valley and Catskill Mountains has been breaking boundaries from the 17th century to today. It was here that American architects first established early residential styles, created mountain resorts and erected the stunning riverside estates that rise from the landscape like its lofty quartz cliffs.

TIMELINE

Pre-European arrival, the Hudson Valley was home to many Indigenous tribes, including the Lenape, Wappinger and Mohican, among others.

1524 ...... First European explorer, Giovanni da Verrazzano, comes to the Hudson Valley

1609 ..... Henry Hudson sails up what will become the Hudson River

1624 ..... Dutch establish Fort Orange, which will become Albany

1686 ...... King of England grants Robert Livingston 160,000 acres. Son expands holding to nearly 500,000.

1704 ..... Traphagen Tavern opens at Ryn Beck crossroads, later named Beekman Arms

1710 ...... German Palatine refugees are settled in the Hudson Valley

1740 ..... First known use of the name "Hudson River"

1788 ...... Ferry connects Catskill and Hudson

1790 ...... "Farmers Turnpike" [today the Milton Turnpike] established to aid transport of apples, peaches and other produce

1797 ...... Hudson comes one vote short of becoming New York's state capital

1819 ...... Last whaling ship sails down the Hudson River

1826 ...... Thomas Cole paints *Kaaterskill Falls*

1851 ...... Hudson River Railroad opens

1872 ...... Frederic Church moves into Olana

1919 ...... Electric refrigeration offers farmers greater flexibility and higher profits

1935 .... Rip Van Winkle Bridge opens

1941 ...... Catskill Mountain House closed, will be burned by New York Conservation Department 1963

1960 ..... Storm King Art Center opens

1976 ...... New York State launches Farm Winery License program

1978 ...... Mooney's Auction founded

2003 ...... Dia:Beacon outpost opens

2009 ..... Hudson-Fulton-Champlain Quadricentennial, the 400th anniversary of Henry Hudson's sail into the river

2017 ...... Family-owned Prospect Hill Orchards celebrates 200 years

2018 ...... Antonio Delgado first Black person and first person of Hispanic descent to be elected to Congress from Upstate New York

2019 ...... Hudson River Skywalk links Olana and Thomas Cole House

FOUNDATIONAL PAINTERS

Noted artists within the Hudson River School.

THOMAS COLE [1801-1848] Founder of the Hudson River School of painting, the first major art movement rooted in America, this lover of landscape was a fierce critic of anything that marred a good view.

....

MARY JOSEPHINE WALTERS [1837-1883] A painter who valued freedom above everything but her art, Walters' meticulously detailed work was inspired by her adventures in the Catskill Mountains.

....

FREDERIC EDWIN CHURCH [1826-1900] An emphasis on composing hyperrealistic scenes led to his signature sorbet-toned sunsets and silvery clouds, while travels in Europe influenced his grand landscapes.

....

EMILY COLE [1843-1913] Intricate painted botanicals on paper and porcelain reveal a keen eye for nature's details, without the grandiosity of the Hudson River School painters her father led.

PAINTED PLACES

Venture into the scenes that inspired famous works.

SUNSET ROCK

Accessed via North-South Lake Campground, one of the most painted views of the Taconic and Berkshire mountains requires some scrambling at the start of a 2.4-mile hike.

KAATERSKILL FALLS

Take a 10-minute hike up to witness this roaring waterfall before setting up a picnic in Kaaterskill Clove, seen in Durand's 1849 *Kindred Spirits*.

CATSKILL MOUNTAIN HOUSE

Demolished in 1963, this site once welcomed guests awed by the grandeur of the Hudson Valley. Read their names carved into the rocks, some dating to the early 1800s.

HUDSON RIVER

The view Joseph Tubby painted in his *Hudson River from Ponckhockie* sits along a short, accessible trail in Kingston's Hasbrouck Park.

HISTORIC HOMES OF NOTE

CLERMONT *Clermont* Family seat of seven generations of Livingstons, the most famous Robert R., who administered Washington's oath of office and developed early steamboat. [1740s]

....

OLANA & THE THOMAS COLE HOUSE *Hudson, Catskill* Homes of teacher [Cole] and student [Church] sit in conversation on opposite sides of the Rip Van Winkle Bridge. Architect autodidact Church, inspired by Middle Eastern buildings, designed Olana himself. [1872 & 1815]

....

PIETER BRONCK HOUSE *Coxsackie* Oldest surviving Upstate home, made of stone with steep-pitched roof. Sits beside 13-sided crimson barn. [1663]

....

BEEKMAN ARMS *Rhinebeck* Sleep where George Washington, Benedict Arnold and Alexander Hamilton dined, drank, likely nursed hangovers. [1704]

....

SPRINGWOOD *Hyde Park* Franklin Delano and Eleanor Roosevelt changed the look of this Italianate estate to Colonial Revival to add more rooms for children. Now home to their presidential library, the very first in U.S. history. [1793]

BUYING TERMS

Fresh	Recently found in a barn or at an estate and has not been presented at auction before. Label relies solely on the honesty of the dealer, so don't take it too seriously.
As Is	Something is wrong, and that's just part of the deal. Pieces offered as is are admittedly flawed but often repairable. Serious patina on true treasures can be polished by a skilled restorer.
Restored/Repaired	Less desirable for collectors, restored or repaired pieces can offer casual buyers a bargain without sacrificing function.
Rare	Take "rare" labels with a grain of salt and run a quick online search before buying to confirm a piece isn't run-of-the-mill or widely reproduced.

CRAFT STYLES

EARLY AMERICAN Pieces from the colonial period and America's early years, typified by having been made in the colonies or states—not imported from Europe. Early painted pieces and rich wood tones are especially desirable.

....

FEDERALIST A 30-year period within Early American [approx. 1789-1823], Federalist styles are what many think of when they hear "antique." This furniture with ties to English neoclassicism can look fuddy-duddy when cramped, but positively contemporary if given room to breathe.

....

MIDCENTURY MODERN Mid-20th century American design movement with clean lines, organic shapes and light wood tones. It's also found new fans in millennials. Furniture names often seen: Eames, Nelson, Knoll, Bertoia.

....

PRIMITIVE The woodshop projects of the past. What unites these pieces is a lack of expertise in execution, but simple shapes and rudimentary designs contribute to sculptural forms with tons of one-of-a-kind character. No defined date range.

DESIGNERS AND PRESERVATIONISTS

Experienced experts on why they live and work in the Hudson Valley.

ROBERT HIGHSMITH & STEFANIE BRECHBUEHLER WORKSTEAD

"At first [our house here] provided a respite from city life. Several chapters later, we renovated this little place when we were expecting our twin girls. In 2018, we moved there full time. Hudson, a short drive away, was a buzzing hub and it's also the site of one of our favorite hotel projects, the Rivertown Lodge. We worked very closely with the owners, along with local and regional craftspeople, on nearly every aspect of the construction. The result is a timeless, iconic hotel that embodies the aesthetic culture of the Hudson Valley and an anchor at the upper end of Warren Street."

....

MARGARET "MARGIE" VERGHESE SET DESIGNER AND DECORATOR

"The most enjoyable part of buying for film and TV sets is research and the hunt for specific styles, moods and eras of furniture and other items. It's fun to work with different decorators, designers and occasionally directors to help them realize their visions through seemingly small everyday objects that become integral to the storytelling."

....

EMILY MAJER WHITE CLAY KILL PRESERVATION

"I think the common theme in what I do as a preservationist, Red Hook's town historian and Tivoli's deputy mayor is community-building. I'm passionate to the point of obsessively nerdy about helping people connect with their homes. Some of my best days are spent in dank 18th-century basements, peering at tool marks and nailheads, praying to find a date stone. I stay up too late reading old deeds and poring over blurry maps. The more you know and understand about your home, your neighborhood, your community, the more context that you have for mapping your place in time and in the world."

....

REBEKAH MILNE AT HOME ANTIQUES & DESIGN

"We found that a lot of people thought antiques weren't for young people, so we have been on a mission to change that. We try to have a wide array of price points for the casual antiquer as well as the serious collector. I love mixing antiques and modern items so that it feels comfortable and contemporary, but still correct for the house."

AUCTION KNOW-HOW

1. Arrive early to inspect the inventory up close. Many Hudson Valley auction houses put up the goods online prior to so you can virtually turn the plates upside down.

2. Set a budget and stick to it. This will help filter what to focus on. But be prepared to spend on hard-to-find items like a Taghkanic basket or painted blanket chest.

3. Remember the buyer's premium—the 11-18 percent additional charge tacked on top of your total.

4. Account for your car. Can those six Shaker chairs really fit in the Subaru? If you can't take it home with you, don't place a bid.

5. Consider starting strong. Calling out 75 percent of your max budget may make others back off.

KEY HOUSES

STAIR GALLERIES *Hudson*
A premiere seller of top collectors' estates across the East Coast, with a focus on art and decorative antiques like silver and porcelain.

MOONEY'S *Freehold*
Go early for the sale, but stay late for the homemade lasagna. This nondescript warehouse in the Catskills has great finds without the pretense.

GEORGE COLE *Red Hook*
Regularly held auctions of all kinds, from vintage toys to high-end furniture to construction equipment. Real estate deals too.

PUBLIC SALE *Hudson*
A new house on the block. Owners Gabriel Constantine and Tarah Gay are big on curation, albeit unorthodox. A welcoming place for bidding newbies to start.

COPAKE AUCTION INC. *Copake*
After hosting their first bicycle auction in 1991, the Fallon family has continued to sell all kinds, from antique big wheels to European racers. Annual swap meet as well.

PERSPECTIVES

"Every time I see the Catskills, or the first fuzz of spring, or 10,000 star-
lings making art in the sky, I feel a slap to the chest. This region does that
for me. Thomas Cole did his darndest to prevent its slide into industrial-
ization and pollution, but we failed to heed the call, of course. 150 years
later, the river was declared a Superfund site. I am tempted to condemn
and dismiss the industrialists, as Cole did, as 'copper-hearted barbarians,'
but then I wince and acknowledge my own guilt. The instinct to both admire and consume nature is in all of us."

—BETSY JACKS, executive director, Thomas Cole National
Historic Site

"The Hudson River Valley has always had an allure that verges on the
mysterious for me. Moving here a decade ago, I was seduced by the mile-
long driveways, idiosyncratic characters, and magnificent architecture
and landscape design. They say that in Newport, Rhode Island, they have
ballrooms, but on the Hudson, we have libraries."

—PIETER ESTERSOHN, photographer, author of *Life Along the Hudson*

"As a Hudson Valley native, I do not believe in any causal connection
between the Hudson Valley and creativity. There isn't something in the
water, or some geomancy vortex that triggers creativity. But there are
a lot of creative people, maybe more than a normal distribution would
suggest. They migrate toward each other, much the way water molecules
join that first ice crystal to become a snowflake."

—VINCENT PIDONE, artist

"Here, art is inescapable. Maybe it's because the art scene isn't tied to any
single college or museum or entity. It isn't institutionalized. It's unstruc-
tured and organic. You have acclaimed artists and musicians living and
working alongside people just starting out. Everyone with their head down
and focused on their work, but also reaching out to mentor and support
and simply exist in the same space as those around them. As I've grown up,
I've learned that's really the sauce of it. We're all participants and patrons
here, and every generation brings something to the table."

—MARIQUITA REESE, brewer, Freehold Art Exchange board member

BESTS

Noted galleries, antique shops and museums.
For more antiques destinations, see page 10.

SALON STYLE

Art Gallery 71
Rhinebeck

Artist-owned gallery forgoes commissions to fully support local creatives. Work hung floor to ceiling.

....

THE VETERAN

Carrie Haddad Gallery
Hudson

Warren Street's original fine-art gallery represents emerging and established talent.

....

OLD SCHOOL

Cold Spring Antiques Center
Cold Spring

What it lacks in rhyme or reason, organizationally speaking, it makes up for in vintage finds.

....

JUNK SHOP

Hodge Podge
Leeds

Many rescue opportunities for sifters, sorters, fixers.

BIG INVENTORY

Coxsackie Antique Center
West Coxsackie

More than 100 dealers in 15,000 sq. ft. Egalitarian ethos: "The antiquing public defines what we carry—not the Madison Avenue interior decorators."

....

DESIGNER'S EYE

FINCH
Hudson

Fashion-industry vet Andrew Arrick and husband Michael Hofemann curate conservatory-like space with refreshing perspective.

....

CAMPUS MUSEUM

Hessel Museum of Art
Annandale-on-Hudson

Rotating cast of contemporary art exhibits at Bard, some student-curated or thesis showings. Open to public.

LIGHTING

Luddite
Germantown

Unassuming garage reveals a glowing trove of lamps, lanterns, schoolhouse pendants, sconces and chandeliers.

....

ITALIAN ART

Magazzino Italian Art
Cold Spring

Cavernous space [*magazzino* means warehouse, after all] celebrates post-War and contemporary Italian art. Gorgeous grounds and research library.

....

FULL SERVICE

Milne Antiques & Design
Kingston

Antiques maven Rebekah Milne's magazine-shoot-worthy showroom. Prop rentals, design consultation and restoration services.

Noted galleries, antique shops and museums.
For more antiques destinations, see page 10.

MIDCENTURY MODERN

Neven & Neven
Moderne
Hudson

OGs that Insta-
brands knock off.
Real-deal Danish
teak, Knoll, Eames.

....

PLACE AS ART

Opus 40
Saugerties

A stone earthwork
over 6.5 acres and 37
years in the making.

....

BIG IDEAS

The School
Kinderhook

FDR-dedicated 1929
high school now
displays cutting-
edge, large-scale
installations.

....

COMMUNITY ART

Tivoli Artists Gallery
Tivoli

Downtown gallery
where 40 painters,
photographers,
sculptors, etc. live
and work.

SALVAGED HISTORY

Zaborski Emporium
Kingston

Everything from
a pair of 8-foot-
tall stained-glass
windows to an 1841
store counter to a
cadre of clawfoots
and stacks of steel
egg baskets.

....

SMALL ACCENTS

Annex Antiques
Red Hook

Approachable, petite
mall ideal for finding
those small pieces
that give a room
character or a pop of
color.

....

CUSTOM FURNITURE

Sawkille Co.
Rhinebeck

Jonah Meyer and
Tara DeLisio hone
and purvey classic
pieces meant to an-
chor a home. Made
with sustainably
forested wood in a
no-waste workshop.

COFFEE & SHOP

Outdated Cafe
Kingston

A cafe in an antique
store or maybe vice
versa. Wildflower-
crowned cakes, vintage
threads, warm lattes,
enamelware dishes.

....

BARN SHOP

A. Therien
Cairo

Crisp gallery with
items both fancy and
folk, plus art books.

....

MOUNTAIN MALL

Tannersville Antiques
Tannersville

Turn-of-the-century
building with 20
booths. Many
cabin-y curios.

....

MAIN STREET MUSEUM

WAAM
Woodstock

Archive of work by
artists who were
part of Woodstock's
unique art colony
heritage.

INTERVIEWS

Ten conversations with locals of note about painting,
historic preservation, small-town life, brewing beer, hardware
stores, farmland access, environmentalism and more

MARYLINE DAMOUR

DESIGNER, ENTREPRENEUR

IN 2012, I read a *New York Magazine* article, and the headline was like, "Hey, you can get this huge, lovely Victorian on 5 acres for $200,000."

IT OCCURRED TO me: I couldn't afford anything in the city, who said I couldn't have a second home before I had the first, right?

SO I HAD a vacation home for five years in Kingston. It propelled me to become an interior designer.

FOR THE FIRST TIME, I had a house where I could paint the walls or demo the bathroom. I wound up selling that house to fund going to Parsons design school.

AFTER I MOVED back here, I spent a year trying to meet other interior designers, makers, architects. It turned out people were not really connected at all.

I DEVELOPED THE Kingston Design Connection's show house because it's the perfect mechanism to bring people together.

I GREW UP seeing Victorian architecture in Haiti. That gingerbread style was actually invented by a Haitian architect who had gone to Paris.

BECAUSE HAITI WAS colonized by the French, I saw interiors with very traditional styles of furniture—lovely turned wood and carved furniture.

KINGSTON'S ONE OF the oldest cities in the country, so our firm, Damour Drake, has worked on many homes from the mid-1800s.

WE OFTEN FIND horse hair and newspaper used as insulation. That was very prevalent.

ONCE, I FOUND an old baby shoe. The Dutch had a practice of putting one in house framing for good luck.

TO COME FACE to face with history on that level, it's so personal.

THIS BELONGED TO someone's baby, and here you are now holding it, 100 years later.

DAN SUAREZ

BREWMASTER

IT STARTED AS a classic American story of brewing at home, brewing in the basement.

AT THE TIME, I was working at a cheese shop in New York City, where I met my wife. I had Tuesday and Wednesday off, so I would go and bother people working at breweries to get experience.

WASH KEGS, SCRUB floors. I had the energy back then.

THE NAME FOR Suarez Family Brewing came after one of my first visits to Belgium.

THESE BREWERIES occupied a larger-than-life space in my head. They have vintage equipment from the late 1800s, a great old building. Everything about it was cool, but what struck me the most is that these breweries are family run and modest.

OUR BREWERY IN Columbia County is a very small one. We don't have a lab. Our analytical tools are on the palate.

WHEN YOU'RE TASTING, you have to train yourself to disassociate from your ego.

WE'LL PLAY A game when we're tasting one of our beers and ask each other, "Where do you want to be when you drink this?"

ALL OF THE fruit we use is whole fruit grown within a 10-minute drive from the brewery.

SOMETIMES I'LL HAVE a farmer turn me on to an ingredient.

THEY'LL ASK, "Oh, you've never tried lemon thyme before?" They bring me some and it starts this inspiration for working it into a beer somehow.

I DID OUR first sweet-cherry beer this year. I went to see the farmer that grows them and drove around his orchard. He let me taste them.

THE BREWERY HAS a simple name, but in that simple name it's evocative of a certain thing. Something grassroots, real.

HEATHER BRUEGL

CULTURAL EDUCATOR

THE FORGE PROJECT is a new organization on the ancestral homeland of Mohican Nations and the Stockbridge-Munsee Community, which I'm a first-line descendant of.

I'M THE NEW director of education there. We provide grants for institutions that are looking to decolonize their programs and create more inclusive learning.

WE WILL BE supporting Indigenous artists and creators who may have a hard time getting into the same venues as non-Native artists.

WE'RE TRYING TO create a playing field that is a little bit more equitable for all.

IN 1609, THE explorer Henry Hudson came sailing down the Mahicannituck, which today we know as the Hudson River. He sailed right into Mohican territory at Castle Island.

WHAT HAPPENED TO the Mohican people there, which is called the Stockbridge-Munsee Community today, was forced movement. We settled near the Housatonic in the Berkshires, which was already part of our territory.

WITH THE AMERICAN Revolution and The War of 1812, more settlers came in. Many nations, if not all, were forced westward.

WITH THE Stockbridge-Munsee we did go back to New York for a brief period, then to Indiana, and finally Wisconsin.

MOVING INTO MY new position with this new organization, I'm very mindful of the land that we're located on and where I will be living.

BEING ABLE TO go home and to be surrounded by my ancestors once again, to see the same vegetation they saw, and to do this work is something very significant.

OUR HOME WILL always and forever be in the Hudson Valley and the Berkshires.

MEL HALES

HARDWARE STORE OWNER

I'M A KID from Harlem. As kids, we played on the Museum Mile. We didn't know we were that broke.

I HAD AN old friend in Newburgh in the '80s. I came up here and saw it was a very good-looking city. I was in my teens and I saw cherry-blossom streets. It was poverty with a view. I was like, "Wow, there's mountains here."

NEWBURGH IS AN idea whose time has come. It's got good bones.

PROGRESS IS COMING, and the cool thing is, there are a lot of decent people who are moving here.

THE HARDWARE STORE is somewhere in the Black community, like the barber shop, the salon. People talk about things. They crossroad it up. I get a microcosm of guys coming in.

AS THE CITY grows, I grow. So I'm pro-city.

THE HARDWARE STORE wasn't my original model for moving here. I came up here to buy property for myself.

MY BACKGROUND WAS in construction. I did architectural drafting. I'm a union carpenter. When I was working on my place, every time I needed something, I made a trip to Home Depot.

IN 2016, a guy said to me, "What the city needs is a damn hardware store." And I thought to myself: It does need a hardware store.

I DIDN'T KNOW retail, but I knew everything about everything that would be in the store.

SOMETIMES YOU GIVE people what they need, not what they want. And I figured they did need it.

IT'S WORKING OUT, and there is a connection to me, being a Black-owned business on Broadway. It's a big deal for some people.

THE STORE HAS a big yellow front. It's bringing light to the gray. We need color down here.

LINDSEY LUSHER SHUTE

FARMER, ADVOCATE

IT WAS ALWAYS a special treat to spend time at my grandfather's farm, in Mercerville, Ohio, which has been in our family for many generations.

HE WAS A full-time Baptist minister, and farming was really a hobby for him.

BUT FOR HIS parents and his parents' parents, it was a full-time job. They were growing for subsistence.

HE WOULDN'T HAVE said he's a farmer, but it was a huge, 2-acre garden. He used his bright orange Allis-Chalmers G tractor, which we have now here with us in the Hudson Valley.

I HAD NO intention of being in agriculture. I actually studied music in undergraduate. But while I was in college, I got into activism and community gardens.

I MOVED TO East Williamsburg. I lived with a couple of friends across from a metal recycling plant. The only sort of oasis on our block was this little community garden that was then gated off.

THAT BOTHERED ME, and I was really stubborn about it. My roommate and I eventually got in there and found all kinds of crazy stuff; we even found a car. We cleaned it up, and it's still an active garden today.

I MET MY husband, Ben, at a rally telling the Bloomberg administration to protect community gardens.

PRETTY SHORTLY AFTER, we moved up to the Hudson Valley to farm full-time. He just didn't have enough space on his rooftop in the city.

THERE WERE SO many challenges we faced in getting our farm, Hearty Roots, off the ground.

WHAT REALLY PUSHED me and Ben to start the National Young Farmers Coalition was this deep frustration with affordable land access, and feeling like this was an even greater obstacle for other farmers who didn't have the same privilege we do.

....

IT WAS SOMETHING that was going to truly prevent young people in the future from pursuing agriculture.

....

LAND PRICES HERE are dictated by an estate value, not what you can earn on the land as a farmer.

....

FARMERS CAN'T COMPETE with someone who might be moving up from the city or tele-commuting who has a much bigger income. So that's really the rub.

....

ONE YEAR, WE had a terrible hailstorm with over 90 percent crop loss. If we were selling to a grocery store or an aggregator, that would have been a huge loss.

....

BUT BECAUSE WE were in this community-supported model, we were in close communication with our customers.

MANY OF THEM even came up to the farm to help us replant.

....

THEY REALLY VIEW it as, "This is where my food comes from. This is my farm too." It showcased the durability of this model. We're not an anonymous grocer.

....

THEY CAN COME see our fields. They can call us up anytime.

....

THE POPULATION GROWTH we've seen over the last year, we need to pair that with opportunity in agriculture, to make sure that we have space for farmers to do well.

....

FARMERS HERE ARE pushing the envelope on innovation. They keep moving the goal post in terms of what it means to have a sustainable small farm.

....

THE HUDSON VALLEY is such an inspiring place to farm because everyone who is doing this work, hard work that doesn't pay a lot, is driven by their sense of purpose in the world.

RICHARD COPPEDGE

CULINARY INSTRUCTOR

AS A TEENAGER, I went from delivering papers to working in a hospital—taking meals up to patients, bringing empty plates back, cleaning the kitchen, taking out the garbage.

THEN THERE WAS an opportunity to do some basic cooking for employee meals, and it started my interest in culinary arts.

I CAME TO the Culinary Institute of America to teach 30 years ago. I have a class called Advanced Baking Principles.

WHEN I CAME here from Johnson & Wales, I was the first person in a long time to come here from that culinary school. I minded my business and let my bread do the talking.

I HAVEN'T TAUGHT bread on a consistent basis in about 20 years, but I still make a nice baguette.

ONE OF THE pioneers in the artisan bread industry, Dan Leader, has a few bakeries in the area called Bread Alone. Before I started here, I had read about him in *Gourmet* magazine.

THE HUDSON VALLEY'S food scene when I started at CIA was pretty basic. If you wanted something unique, you went to Westchester or New York City.

NOW YOU DON'T have to just go to Woodstock to get good vegetarian food. There are 20-some restaurants in the Rhinebeck area, which only has one traffic light.

MORE THAN FIVE of my former students are on the faculty here. They're now my colleagues.

I GO TO Market Street in Rhinebeck, where the owner is a former teacher. I don't advertise that I'm coming there, but if a former student recognizes me while I'm there, they call him and he says, "Send out six desserts."

IT'S NICE—they want me to try them. I'm appreciative of their respect.

NORA LAWRENCE

CURATOR

I WAS EXCITED to get this job at Storm King Art Center in no small part because of my history of coming here as a kid.

I GREW UP in New York City and spent summers coming up to Monroe most of my life.

I REMEMBER ROLLING down the hills. I remember Richard Serra and his beautiful piece, *Schunnemunk Fork*. From the first time I saw that, it was absolutely a favorite of mine.

STORM KING IS a place where people feel really free as they see artwork. I wanted to be a part of that.

HAVING THE NEW York State Thruway run past here could be seen as a negative, but I think about it as the connection to how these lands were parceled and put together to create the site we have.

STORM KING HAS been a long-term reclamation project to bring the natural beauty of the region back to the landscape. We started out with 22 acres; now we're at 500.

WE MOVED FROM the museum building that's on top of the hill out into the fields by always following the will of artists, which I think is beautiful.

SARAH SZE'S *Fallen Sky* is spherical, and it's a 36-foot-diameter work. I think it's amazing that it's both large-scale and almost invisible. It has a mirrored surface.

IT GIVES BACK to the environment.

YOU CAN SEE it from the furthest reaches of the property.

AND YET IT has no height to it. It doesn't break the horizon line of the hill that it's on.

I THINK IT'S important Storm King takes on the challenge of representing many different experiences with nature, and what art can be within it.

LEONG ONG AND PHILIP LEEMING

DESIGNERS

LO: I grew up in Malaysia and was fortunate to go to boarding school in the U.K. at 14. From there, I developed my interest in art and design.

LO: Clothing gives you a certain power of expression. I found that in painting and drawing, but fashion felt more sculptural.

PL: I'm from the North of England. I was the only person in my super working-class family to go to university. I worked in Italy for six years and came to New York to work for Anne Klein in '97.

PL: I had no idea it was an old lady brand before I moved here. I met Leong about five months later.

LO: Back in the '90s, New York was this shining sort of city, almost an Oz-like place. I worked at Ralph Lauren for a few years. I got my fill and left.

LO: We started coming to a rental not far from here. In hindsight, if we hadn't done that, I don't think I'd be in New York anymore. The city is amazing, but I needed greenery.

PL: When we first came up here, I was just getting to know Leong. I fell in love with him up here.

LO: You realize that this is something you need as a tonic to the hustle and bustle.

LO: The Falls brand was originally vintage clothing I embroidered, but we've also started doing home goods.

PL: I feel like in my corporate job, I'm not creating a lot of the time, so I'll jump in on what he's doing and say, "Can I just design some embroideries, please?"

LO: We've always traveled so much that our house was enough for us. But lately we rediscovered the amazing Mohonk trails and Minnewaska State Park.

PL: It's changed so much in 20 years, but it's still inspiring to meet the people who live and work up here.

LOUISE COOPER SMITH

ARTIST

HUDSON IS AN incredibly small city, which is what I love about it. My studio is on the main drag, Warren Street.

I'M ON THE top floor of an antique store. I can see a church steeple and the bank from my window. It's really picturesque.

HUDSON IS BEAUTIFUL in the sense that you will bump into somebody who you haven't seen in awhile. And that can be an opportunity for any discussion, but also sparking engagement and new projects with new people.

IF YOU'RE SOMEBODY like me who's a bit more of an introvert, that's a really special thing.

PAINTING IS INCREDIBLY solitary, which is why I've been drawn to it. I was always a pretty shy kid, and painting and drawing was a very meditative, safe, peaceful space for me.

I START BY getting most of my materials from the hardware store. The paint comes in after.

I'VE ALWAYS BEEN drawn to texture. I've been working on these paintings where I'm pushing spackle through window screens, and then painting on top of the surface. It gives the pixelated look and feel of a textile.

MY GRANDMOTHER was a researcher at The Met in New York City. She's in her 90s now and just stopped working there.

ON MONDAYS, ALL the workers could go to the galleries for free. I have these memories of going with her and having my mind blown, drawing in a notebook.

I DON'T KNOW if I would say it's so much that I feel like a Hudson River Valley artist, as much as I feel like I just really love the community that I'm in and I want to be a part of that. I don't want to just show work here, but also give back in some ways.

I HOPE THAT my work can strike curiosity within people who live in my community and I can learn from them.

JON BOWERMASTER

FILMMAKER

THERE ARE MORE environmental activists per capita in the Hudson Valley than anywhere in the country.

IN THE '50S and '60s, when environmental threats haunted the Hudson, the American environmental movement was born here to fight against power plants planning to build on the shores.

I WAS FREELANCING in 1988, and I knew I wanted to be surrounded by green more than cement. I moved to Stone Ridge, which was a sleepy little village then. No traffic lights. Now we have three.

FOR THE LAST 20 years, I've focused on documentaries with environmental backdrops.

I MADE FILMS on every continent, but six years ago I decided you don't have to travel around the world to find environmental stories. There were a lot here.

WE MADE A series called *River at Risk*. But I got bummed out because I thought, I'm just telling stories about potential horrors. I don't want that to be my sole subject matter.

WE PURPOSELY pivoted and made *Hope on the Hudson*, which are more optimistic stories.

SOMETIMES I THINK we're a little spoiled. Most regions don't have this preponderance of successful environmental groups.

I DRIVE ACROSS the river almost daily. Because of the clouds, the Catskill Mountains, the river itself, it looks different every time.

BUT THEN I remind myself the Hudson River is also the country's largest Superfund site.

SOMETIMES THERE'S A price to pay for knowing too much.

I WORK WITH environmental groups to improve access. A lot of land along the river is private.

I THINK ONE thing that helps preserve places is if people are using them.

ANN MARIE GARDNER

MAGAZINE FOUNDER, ENTREPRENEUR

AFTER GRADUATE SCHOOL, I moved to London and started writing about health trends. A friend happened to invite me to lunch with the editor of *Tatler*.

THIS IS THE late '90s. I was growing a kombucha mushroom in my house. I was doing wheatgrass. She was just amazed, and she goes, "Could you write me a three-part series?"

AFTER I MOVED back to the States, I came up here to do a story on Gun and Martina who started FACE Stockholm. They moved their headquarters here because this is the same landscape as Sweden.

THIS PLACE RESONATED with me so much. I fell in love with it. I rented Martina's barn in Germantown.

BACK THEN, WHEN I'd go out to eat with my assistant and her foodie friends in the city, they were like, "I need to know where that chicken came from." When I traveled, people would say, "You live in the country? Do you have chickens? Goats?"

EVERYBODY WAS REALLY into the country and where their food came from.

I THOUGHT, "THIS is so weird. Is it a story?" And then I thought, "This is actually a movement that's about to happen."

I WAS NOTICING the scene up here, and it was a little bit like *Portlandia*—the Young Farmers Coalition in their sweaters with their beards and their flannels. I thought it was funny.

SO I WROTE a screenplay called *Upstate*. One of the characters in the show was a magazine editor.

I CALLED UP a guy I knew in television, and he said, "That's not happening." And I'm like, "No, it's happening. I'm living it. Don't tell me it's not happening."

THEN I WAS like, "Why don't I just make a magazine?" In 15 min-

utes, I wrote the table of contents. I wound up raising money for it.

ONE OF MY writers, Jesse Hirsch, did that story, "So, You Want to Be a Farmer?"

HE DECIDED, "NO, I don't want to be a farmer. It's really hard." And it is. A lot of people made it, but a lot of people didn't.

FARMING weeds out the poseurs.

IT'S BEEN ALMOST a decade since. I think we definitely put "modern farming" into the vernacular. The timing was just right.

IF WE STARTED *Modern Farmer* today, it probably would be a Netflix series. Definitely a newsletter, right?

STORIES

_Essays and selected writing by noted
voices from the Hudson Valley & Catskills_

MY JANE AUSTEN LIFE

Written by **RUTH REICHL** | **WANT TO WRITE ME A LETTER?** If you simply address it to "Ruth, Spencertown, New York," I'll probably get it.

When I walk into the quaint little post office in our town, the postmistress will hand it over saying, "This came for you." Then Kate will rewrap the package I'm mailing [I never do it well enough to suit her] while filling me in on the latest news about the softball team.

That's what I love about living here.

Some mornings I wake up, stare at the mist rising off the mountains and try to figure out how I wandered into this Jane Austen life. For a person raised in the studied anonymity of a Manhattan apartment building [my parents lived next door to the same couple for 40 years without ever knowing their names], it is comforting to be part of a community where privacy is impossible. We even have what amounts to a local squire: the artist Ellsworth Kelly lived in our little hamlet for a large part of his life, and although he's no longer with us, his husband, Jack Shear, continues to support every local cause. They built us a fire station, renovated Town Hall and maintained conservancy trails; at Christmas, Jack even goes around town handing out Champagne. And yes, we all watch his comings and goings with the kind of avid curiosity so often found in Austen books—and so rarely in American cities. I know a lot about neighbors I have never met—and they know a lot about me.

A couple years ago I stupidly lit a fire without opening the vent in the fireplace. Five minutes later, I was doing my best to evict the billows of smoke that filled the house when the fire chief showed up. "I know your husband is away," said this man I'd never met before, "and when the alarm went off, I thought I'd better stop in and make sure you were alright."

When we moved here 30 years ago I had no idea it would be like this. But not a week had passed before a neighbor phoned to say he was certain we had old friends in common. "You don't know me," he began, "but the postmistress told me about you. Why don't you come over for dinner?"

Sadly, they were vegetarians. Our nearest neighbor, however, was not. That first fall, we were startled to come home and find a deer carcass hanging outside Kenny's house. The next day there were more. And more. Kenny took hunting season seriously, using a bow and arrow [the season is longer] so he could fill the freezer with meat for the year. When Kenny heard that I write about food [it was probably the postmistress who told him], he began showing up with packages of meat. Venison, duck, even wild turkey, although he didn't think much of the poor birds. "Dry and bony," was his assessment, "but they make decent chili. Here, I'll give you the recipe."

In those days people around here tended to be frugal. Wealthy weekenders went to chic places like the Hamptons, leaving our valley to families who had been here for generations. They tolerated the artists, writers and musicians who'd been drawn by the untamed beauty of the land and its startlingly low cost. There was also, of course, a sprinkling of cooks, thrilled to be surrounded by farmers. We shopped local, rarely went out to eat [where would you go?]and never dressed up.

Friends who came to visit were mostly in search of bargains in Hudson's many antique shops. We'd spend days walking down Warren Street, going in and out of funky little storefront places where the proprietors huddled over heaters—the shops were always freezing—and offered an astonishingly varied collection of goods. It was an endless treasure hunt. After a couple of years, the dealers all knew I collected old kitchen implements, and they'd call whenever something interesting arrived. My greatest find was an antique juicer that resembles an elephant. It cost two dollars.

Afterward, we'd wander off Warren to the adjacent streets, whose once-magnificent buildings had turned into wrecks. I always took people past the imposing Colonial Revival house on Court Street where the poet John Ashbery lived, hoping we might get a glimpse of the great man. We never did, but we'd eye the beautiful ruins around his home and wonder if they were affordable.

A few years ago it hit me that the wrecks were disappearing; by now all the beautiful buildings in Hudson have been restored to their former glory. The antique shops are mostly gone, replaced by restaurants, clothing stores and wine shops patronized by the inhabitants of these now-stately homes. Things are also starting to change here in our little

town. We have a fine new performance space, and it looks like we're going to have a Shaker museum. There's great local cheese, eager young farmers, talented bakers. New restaurants seem to open every day. It all became too much for Kenny. A few years ago he sold his house to an artist who has replaced the hanging deer with contemporary sculptures. The air is still filled with the raucous sound of gunshots during hunting season, but I suspect the people in bright-red jackets are here for sport rather than survival.

Change, of course, is inevitable. But I'm already nostalgic for the life we're losing.

Each time I pass the charming old church on our town green, I notice the sign that says it has been here since 1772. It reminds me that what I love most about living here is how slowly things changed in the intervening years. But things are speeding up. Any day now I'll wake to find that I'm surrounded by strangers—and that envelopes addressed to Ruth in Spencertown have been returned to sender.

RUTH REICHL lives in the Hudson Valley because she thinks it's the best place for a cook in the country. And she should know: she was the food editor of the *Los Angeles Times*, the restaurant critic of *The New York Times* and the last editor of *Gourmet* magazine.

COUNTRY TWITTER

Written by SANDY ALLEN

BEFORE MOVING OUT HERE, to the Western Catskills, I had rarely seen a sunrise. Nor had I contemplated the difference between *dawn* [dusk's counterpart] and *sunrise* itself, that moment when the sun becomes visible on the horizon. I've been here four years now, and, in that time, I've felt myself rising earlier and earlier. Meaning, these days, I catch the sunrise pretty often. Before living here, I admit I didn't know at all about what happens that time of day, birds-wise—an event I've since learned that bird people call the "dawn chorus."

It'll begin around first light, with maybe just one bird calling, over and over. Then a few more birds will join. The light will continue to grow, as will the song, more and more birds adding their calls. I'll hear robins, blackbirds, crows. I'll hear the rooster at the farm down the valley. I'll hear the "hey sweetie, hey sweetie" of a chickadee and a woodpecker going "tap, tap, tap" on a sugar maple. The light swells as does the sound, until, at last, everything builds to that rapturous climax: the sun.

Then the birdsong wanes. The day has begun.

More than just a chorus, I've thought, this event is the birds' overture, a sonic preview of everybody singing in the region that day. Lately, I notice how the sound shifts with the seasons as our bird populations do. In autumn and spring, so many migrate through here that my pond becomes a popular avian Airbnb, hosting numerous pairs of ducks and sometimes large gaggles of geese, with their noise and mess and adorable fuzzy goslings. On some spring mornings, the dawn chorus will be so loud with so many different birds, it'll amaze me it doesn't wake up everybody.

In midwinter, on the other hand, I'll walk my dog up the ridge and pause at the top, in the dark cold, and listen for birds. I'll hear crows, maybe a few others. My dog will protest, yearning for his bed by the fire. The light rises slowly until the orange orb finally appears above the peaks. Sometimes it'll only be the crows calling, as it does. They are our most constant neighbors here, the crows.

We've got about four or five that are always hanging around. I watch them as they argue in the aspens or filch apples from the orchard. When the temperatures are frigid and snows deep, they perch on the still-green spruces and chat amongst themselves. I have wondered what the crows think of all the transient birds who fly through for a spell or a season, all those babbling songbirds and waterfowl who stay for the warm months, who make that dawn chorus such a racket. I wonder if the crows prefer company or peace. Perhaps, like me, they enjoy the way this place shifts with the seasons, in some ways encouraging community-building, and in others, solitude.

Catskills locals sometimes call outsiders "flatlanders," and I think that's telling, that they've made a binary that is them versus the world. I do understand the sense that it is different up here in these steep green folds of the mountains. There is a strange and even mystical feeling here. A sense that time *is* different or we've traveled backward. There's a coziness in that feeling, a comfort too. And an intensity. The way people act up here threw me off, at first. How someone might show up at 7 a.m. on a Saturday to commence a project discussed years before. How folks like to pull over and say hi, or linger and ask lots of questions. When we were brand new, the line of inquiry often felt like, "How are you planning on surviving, up here?"

Now, I'm the one who frets when visitors come, explaining to them the machinations of ticks or warning how severe and unpredictable the weather can be. I caution them to download their maps before heading out because there's often no service on these winding roads. If a friend gets stung by a hornet or encounters a snake, I'll notice how, for them, this is out of the ordinary; to me, this has become mundane.

Maybe this is my attraction to the dawn chorus, why it so entrances me. It serves as a good reminder that my little vantage is but one way of seeing. Living up here, so close to nature, I'm often humbled by the smallness of my position in the scheme of everything. I'm often reminded how much anything can shift. Including how we see our own worlds.

Apparently scientists don't have a consensus as to why the birds sing at sunrise; there are various theories.

I'll add mine.

The birds are saying, "HOORAY, it's the sun!!! We are ALIVE! Here on this glorious rock! What a gift, this day!"

SANDY ALLEN is a transgender writer who lives in the Catskills. He's the author of *A Kind of Mirraculas Paradise: A True Story about Schizophrenia* [Scribner]. More at *hellosandyallen.com*.

EDNA ST. VINCENT MILLAY

AUTUMN DAYBREAK

Cold wind of autumn, blowing loud
At dawn, a fortnight overdue,
Jostling the doors, and tearing through
My bedroom to rejoin the cloud,
I know—for I can hear the hiss
And scrape of leaves along the floor—
How may boughs, lashed bare by this,
Will rake the cluttered sky once more.
Tardy, and somewhat south of east,
The sun will rise at length, made known
More by the meager light increased
Than by a disk in splendor shown;
When, having but to turn my head,
Through the stripped maple I shall see,
Bleak and remembered, patched with red,
The hill all summer hid from me.

THE BUCK IN THE SNOW

White sky, over the hemlocks bowed with snow,
Saw you not at the beginning of evening the antlered buck and his doe
Standing in the apple-
orchard? I saw them. I saw them suddenly go,
Tails up, with long leaps lovely and slow,
Over the stone-wall into the wood of hemlocks bowed with snow.

Now lies he here, his wild blood scalding the snow.

How strange a thing is death, bringing to his knees, bringing to his antlers
The buck in the snow.
How strange a thing,—a mile away by now, it may be,
Under the heavy hemlocks that as the moments pass
Shift their loads a little, letting fall a feather of snow—
Life, looking out attentive from the eyes of the doe.

EDNA ST. VINCENT MILLAY (1892-1950) was a Pulitzer Prize-winning, internationally famous writer and poet known as much for embodying a liberated, modern woman in the Jazz Age as for her work. Millay wrote both of these poems at Steepletop, her residence in Austerlitz, New York, which is now home to the Millay Society. To learn more visit *www.millay.org*

DIRECTORY & INDEX

DIRECTORY

ART MUSEUMS & SPACES

Art Gallery 71 *Rhinebeck*
Art Omi *Ghent*
Basilica Hudson *Hudson*
Bearsville Theater *Woodstock*
Bethel Woods Center for the Arts *Bethel*
Carrie Haddad Gallery *Hudson*
Dia:Beacon *Beacon*
Hessel Museum of Art *Annandale-on-Hudson*
Howland Cultural Center *Beacon*
Magazzino Italian Art *Cold Spring*
Manitoga *Garrison*
Morphicism *Beacon*
Mother Gallery *Beacon*
Opus 40 *Saugerties*
The School *Kinderhook*
Storm King Art Center *New Windsor*
Thomas Cole National Historic Site *Catskill*
Tivoli Artists Gallery *Tivoli*
Woodstock Artists Association
    and Museum *Woodstock*

LODGING

Batterby House *Hudson*
Callicoon Hills *Callicoon Center*
The DeBruce *Livingston Manor*
Deer Mountain Inn *Tannersville*
The Graham & Co. *Phoenicia*
Hotel Kinsley *Kingston*
Hotel Tivoli *Tivoli*
Hutton Brickyards *Kingston*
Inness House *Accord*
Mohonk Mountain House *New Paltz*
The Red Rose Motel *Roscoe*
Rivertown Lodge *Hudson*
The Roundhouse *Beacon*
Scribner's Catskill Lodge *Hunter*
Spruceton Inn *West Kill*
The Stewart House *Athens*
Sylvan Motor Lodge *Hillsdale*
Troutbeck *Amenia*
Urban Cowboy *Big Indian*
Woodstock Way *Woodstock*

SHOPS & ANTIQUE STORES

A. Therien *Cairo*
Annex Antiques Center *Red Hook*
The Antique Warehouse *Hudson*
Batterby House *Hudson*
Beacon Mercantile *Beacon*
Beekman Arms Antique Market *Rhinebeck*
Clove & Creek *Kingston*
Cold Spring Antiques Center *Cold Spring*
Cold Spring General Store *Tannersville*
Coxsackie Antique Store *Coxsackie*
Demitasse *Millerton*
Dette Flies *Livingston Manor*
FINCH *Hudson*
Hodge Podge Shop *Leeds*
Hoffman's Barn *Red Hook*
Inquiring Minds Bookstore *New Paltz*
Kingston Consignments *Kingston*
Luddite *Germantown*
Mary MacGill *Germantown*
Milne Antiques & Design *Kingston*
Neven & Neven Moderne *Hudson*
Outdated Cafe *Kingston*
Quittner Antiques *Germantown*
Sundry. *Tannersville*
SWING *Cold Spring*
Tannersville Antiques *Tannersville*
Tivoli Mercantile *Tivoli*
Westerlind *Millerton*
WYLDE Hudson *Hudson*
Zaborski Emporium *Kingston*

BOOKSHOPS

Barner Books *New Paltz*
Blenheim Hill Books *Hobart*
Oblong Books *Rhinebeck*
Postmark Books *Rosendale*
The Golden Notebook *Woodstock*
Magpie Bookshop *Catskill*
Rodgers Book Barn *Hillsdale*
Rough Draft Bar & Books *Kingston*
Split Rock Books *Cold Spring*
Spotty Dog *Hudson*

INDEX

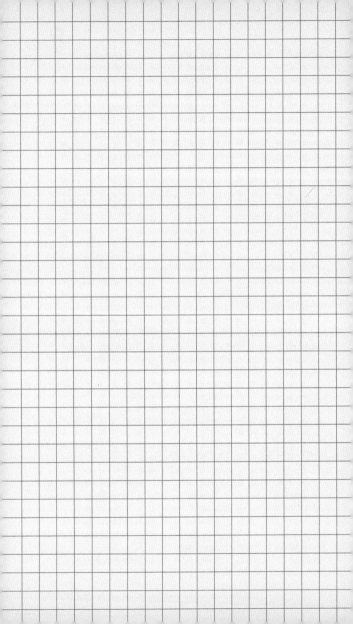

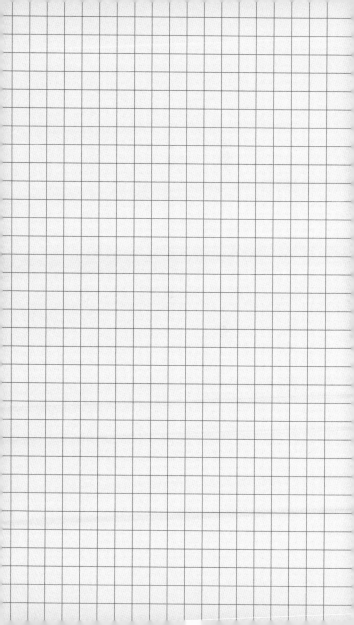

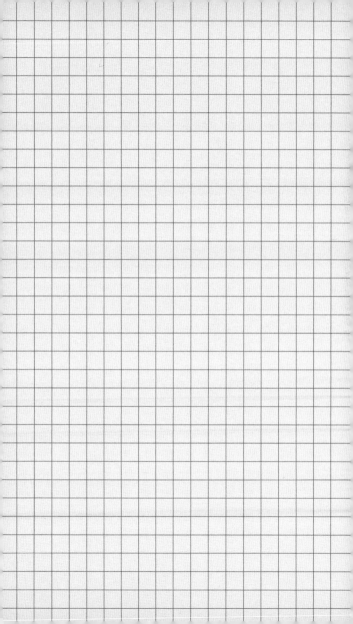

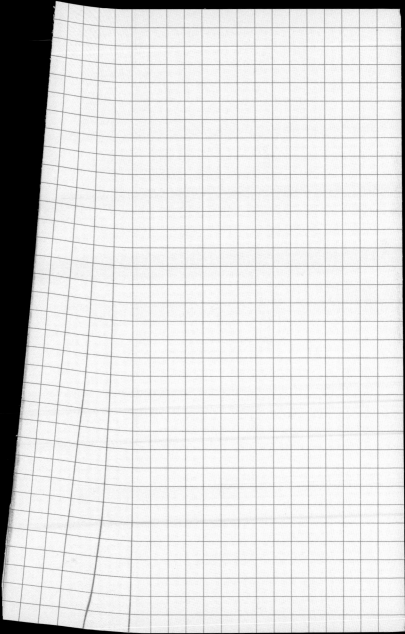

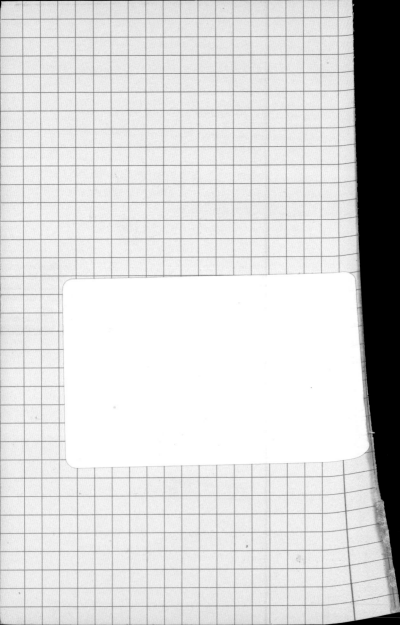